INVESTMENT PROPERTIES

Building Wealth through Investment Properties

by

Evelyn Harden

AF722137

DORRANCE PUBLISHING CO
EST. 1920
PITTSBURGH, PENNSYLVANIA 15238

The contents of this work, including, but not limited to, the accuracy of events, people, and places depicted; opinions expressed; permission to use previously published materials included; and any advice given or actions advocated are solely the responsibility of the author, who assumes all liability for said work and indemnifies the publisher against any claims stemming from publication of the work.

Dorrance Publishing Co
585 Alpha Drive
Suite 103
Pittsburgh, PA 15238
Visit our website at *www.dorrancebookstore.com*

ISBN: 979-8-8860-4154-5
eISBN: 979-8-8860-4810-0

Contents

Introduction

Have you ever thought of owning a multifamily home?

This book is my memoirs on my trek through purchasing and maintaining multifamily dwellings. On the way I helped others secure their dreams also. Owning properties is one path toward increasing your financial security. Everything I will tell you about investing in multifamily properties can be easily discovered. In fact, with Google everything is at your fingertips. If this is your dream—just do it. Watch the market. Markets are always changing. Take a fresh look. Read the Real Estate ads, and the Classifieds for Rentals and Sale ads. Drive through the rental neighborhoods and new construction areas and get a feel for it. Trust your thoughts and your judgment. Everybody has advice, but You are your own best ally. Professional people will be there to help you but check it all out yourself first. Get a feel for it all. Then get your ducks in a row and go meet the people I will introduce you to in the following pages.

Someone once said, "The School of Hard Knocks can be feared or enjoyed." I'm one of the 70% of Americans who did not finish college. College is one advantage, I truly believe in, and owning a multifamily home can help ease your burden if you are looking for a way to decrease your personal expenses to increase your disposable income. Basically, I have not paid rent or utilities for 20 years. My journey from start to finish was sort of like the School of Hard Knocks at times. I felt I was stepping into someone else's world, one I had little or no experience in. But then what is learning if you can't take a chance? And if you never squeeze lemons, you will never taste lemonade.

Who me? We were homesteaders in Alaska in the years preceding statehood when 160-acre parcel homesteads were offered to entice citizens to populate the state, as many young families with similar means, settled here to start new lives. As young adults, Mom and Dad left everything and traveled with three toddlers to secure a 160-acre parcel in Homer, Alaska. As it was told to me, they registered for the parcel with the intent to move on to it and survive one year. The requirements were to survive in a livable home, have a water source and prove up on the property. At that point the parcel became theirs and Alaska became their home.

Alaska holds unique attractions. More than its rich resources, rugged beauty and sparse population is the continually changing lengths of days. Solstices are much more extreme here. The winter daylight hours are short. Nights get longer and darker until the Winter Solstice in December, but long dark nights continue into January and February. Winds howl and snow flies in feisty blizzards, which can leave as quickly as they appear, frequently clearing to a beautiful blue sky and a blanket of fresh white snow and even though the snow stays frozen, the air feels warm. It's Christmas card weather!

March, chosen in Alaska as the month of the *Iditarod* because of the abundance of glistening white snow that falls softly through the night covering everything. Longer days and milder temperatures come as the Spring Equinox passes. Then April is Spring Breakup and as days continue to lengthen, rain melts the snow, and the ground turns to mud. All vegetation is brown and bare except for the dark hues of the evergreens. The deep indigo blue snow-capped mountains across the bay, border the shimmering blue water and are sometimes lighted from behind by the Northern Lights.

Winter or summer, the views of the mountains surrounding the bay take your breath away, but May is a month to behold! Now it's warm! Nature is abundant. On May 1, as the mornings and evenings stretch into the night, and the spring breezes fill the air, the trees show the first shoots of green. It's like a time-lapse, from that day till Memorial Day, the trees unfurl at an unbelievable pace. Vegetation springs up exuberantly, free from the confinement of winter and explodes into a wonderland of a plush green thicket, where leaves are so thick you can't see ten feet in front of you. Indigo mountains, still surround the bay, but now they cling to wispy bits of snow and ice, that hangs like lace from their rugged peaks. The sun shines in a bright blue sky. The birds sing—even at 2:00 am—if you go outside, it is warm, the sun is up, and the birds are singing. And everything is peaceful. Moose are still seen in early mornings and late evenings, often with newborn calves, taking advantage of the early growth in lower altitudes, while the snow is still deep in the mountains. Birds fly back home while squirrels and other wildlife emerge from hibernation. Everything is alive, moving, growing,

June is summer--fair and sunny all night. The sun which rises in the north-northeast, circles the sky and sets in the north-northwest, seems to always be 10:00 am or 4:00 pm. Wild roses spread across the landscape, as well as geraniums, lupines, and fireweed, adding huge splashes of color to the green plushness as in July and August wild berries ripen and skies are set aflame during late evening sunsets. Summer settles down in September with crisp sunny days and frosted nights, and frequently by Halloween we'll see a glistening blanket of fresh white snow. December has the shortest days of the year, where the sun rises in the southeast, arcs slightly and sets in the southwest. Here again, it's 10:00 am to 4:00 pm, but those are the actual hours from sunup to sundown in Homer. Alaska is legendary for the uniqueness of the equinoxes and solstices, the long dark winter nights, and bright sunny nights in summer.

Arriving in early summer, my parents began the task of setting up the new life. As they progressed toward winter, they were living in a 15-foot trailer with three very small children, when Mom discovered once again, she was pregnant. What's more, long about Christmas as her due date neared, she began to suspect twins! As her time drew near in February, she boarded a small plane piloted by the same doctor who would deliver me. My twin brother was child number four, and I was number five. A week later the same doctor flew the three of us home to meet the rest of our family. Our family grew as two more baby girls joined us within the next few years.

The home I remember most had a large wood stove in the living area. Five-gallon buckets full of snow were set atop it to melt for drinking water, cooking, cleaning, and bathing. As the snow melted, a dipper was hung from the inside rim. Freshly melted snow makes delicious drinking water. This was the first half of my childhood, growing up in a small town of about 200 families—and we were all pretty much in the same boat. Those of us on the outskirts of town had no electricity or running water. Mom and Dad lit butane lanterns in the evening. Evening entertainment was limited to family stories and popcorn, since Homer did not receive a television signal, radio waves from Anchorage were often weak, and batteries were expensive. Overall, it was like a lifelong camping trip.

Then suddenly it changed. The spring I turned eleven, we picked up and moved to Eastern Oregon, where I started sixth grade. I felt like an alien that had flown in from outer space and was trying to integrate into the crowd. Not all was bad. I fell in love and suffered my first broken heart and gradually I blended in, but life was different, and people thought differently. My family had not even owned a car much of the time in Alaska. We had ridden the school bus, but now we walked to school, and Mom drove to work. We soon learned to appreciate the wooded beauty, sunny weather, and warm summer nights in Oregon, as well as the benefits of living in town. We were home again.

I was a precocious teenager who preferred working and earning money to doing chores and schoolwork. During my junior high years, I worked babysitting and cleaning house for local families. It was by choice. Mom wouldn't let me take an official babysitting job until I was thirteen, which only added to the enchantment of it. My older sisters seemed so mature using their own money to buy fashionable clothes, makeup, toiletries, and hair products. They moved around in clouds of luxurious smelling fragrances, and could buy the sexy toothpastes and shampoos, seen in the commercials where beautiful models danced with hair soft and shiny. Making money for a few hours of doing something in charge felt really grownup. Babysitting jobs were plenteous in our small town. We accepted the wage offered without question. The best jobs were the ones where the young mother steps back into the workforce, leaving three or four children with a sitter. These were steady and reliable, sometimes paid less per hour but valuable because of steady employment. Wages were very low and babysitting hours can be grueling, although playing with children is not a bad pastime. And after they go to sleep, we could sleep ourselves, so weeknights were allowed. We had nothing better to do really, and it kept us out of mischief. But the money, as well as the status was power, and the more hours you invested, the more money you took home. The admirations of friends were as welcome as the wages. My sister and I became very popular in the babysitting world and soon were passing off jobs to our friends. We had a pretty good referral system going but then I moved to a new city.

Still in Oregon but a new high school, everything was different now. My contacts and referral system were absent. I applied at every restaurant and motel in town for a services job, but with no experience, I didn't have much luck. One restaurant agreed to hire me in the kitchen, but I would work school nights till after 10:00 pm and come home dirty. I wouldn't be in bed till midnight, and I doubted that I could get up and be functional at school. Still, I was game but then someone suggested I apply at a local state employment office. Through a government sponsored program, I secured a part-time office position in a government personnel office! They had a dress code and structured office proceedings. I had my own desk! Wages were ridiculously low—lower than minimum wage since we were still in high school--and hours were limited. I could work fulltime in the summers and part time in winters, to facilitate school attendance. This was an enviable upgrade! Although I still funded most of my personal upkeep—mostly by choice—I saved parsimoniously and had bought a new, used car the fall I started my senior year. I was feeling real grown up. And although I bought most of my own clothes, lunches, and funded my social life, and now had a car, I had never questioned real expenses like groceries, rent, utilities or mortgage payments. Forget mortgage payments, one rent payment and groceries were more than I made in one month! It had never occurred to me how much overhead expenses would be! And college was never really in the cards for me. It wasn't something my family talked about. And frankly, the thought of four additional years of studying and struggling with bills was daunting. There were no plans, funds, or approaches that looked feasible. Choosing a life partner and thinking it was magic, as a 17-year-old, I jumped into marriage.

A decade later, tired of low paying jobs, now a mother with young children, I reevaluated my education and spent a year in business college. I had learned a whole new appreciation for education, graduated with high marks at age 28 and began a new career on the lower rungs of the business world. Although I would not trade my humble beginnings, I am thankful every day that I am an American and it is my right and responsibility to move on.

My income had risen and now tripled the existing minimum wage, and that may sound good but in Oregon, with two dependent children, my children actually qualified for reduced school lunch fees. That was a big help but the cost of living was always a struggle and a little out of reach. It became painfully clear that a job was not enough. After my divorce, I enrolled again in classes at the local community college working toward a degree, mostly night classes, but I finally called a halt to it. I needed to spend more time with my family. Instead of school, I began reading books directed at raising income. The first books I read were encouraging but not so simple. One book suggested owning a whole subdivision. Great book with many great principles I still rely on today—but unless you have a cash windfall or are a builder yourself—it doesn't seem possible. Still, it alluded to the possibility, and I enjoyed the book so much, I read everything else I could find on the subject. Even the realtors' ads touting, *Stop Throwing Your Money Away on Rent.*

I had toyed with the idea before, curiously watching other landlords. This sounded like a great answer, I reasoned it would make my house payment, clearly the largest payment I had. Although it would be another seven years before I bought my first multifamily home, that was when I set out to become a landlord. This was a whole new career, and the education could be gained with everyday events like reading books, attending seminars, watching the market, and reading the local newspaper.

Investment Properties Are Not a *Get Rich Quick* Scheme…

- They supplement/pay your mortgage payment and utilities bills
- Or provide a stable supplemental income
- Self-employment; Part-time flexible hours
- Build equity for college or retirement wealth

Time To Think Critically

When you buy a multifamily property, you buy a business, and you are the owner and manager. Investing in rental properties is not a *get rich quick* scheme but can provide security and prove to be a solid supplement for future needs, such as college tuition, self-employment, or retirement income, for only a few dedicated hours a month. By renting your property to accommodate others, the income will cover or reduce your mortgage payment, usually the largest expense you have! Their rent will pay either your rent or a mortgage payment every month for as long as you own them! How you manage it will determine how much of your current income this will free up.

Whatever your reason to initiate such a purchase, it is a life-changing event and management training is part of the course. This is a business and must be run like one.

You purchased a building, but you now own a business.

Whether it works for you or not, depends on how you run it! Investing in a multifamily can be surprisingly inexpensive to get started. It can return profits immediately, and it must if you want to succeed! You take all responsibility. It is all yours, yours to make or break. What happens, happens to you and your lender, and everyone else walks away.

Look around your community and you will see that a lot of people purchase and successfully run multifamily homes in various capacities. Multifamily homes, for FHA and VA loan purposes, cannot exceed four units but can vary in quality and value from large and expensive to small and quite modest. Not all units in the same property must be equal in size; an *owner's* unit is common, and in some cases, units may not necessarily even be attached. Some appear well cared for and others *age* quickly! Some stay rented and others sit empty.

But what if you are diligent, learn the applicable law and follow fair business practices with integrity? So many things are on your side, there to help you. The immediate *return on investment* (ROI) to you is reduced or free rent in exchange for a part-time job.

Transitioning into retirement, becoming, or supporting a full-time student can be greatly eased by owning a home which makes its own payment, since your mortgage expense is the largest payment you make. For that matter, a young parent who wishes to stay home and care for children would also fare well while supplementing the family income. Surviving on unemployment compensation payments through the off seasons seems to take place annually with some jobs, and if you are in a commissioned job, the inequality of commissioned sales work can be less painful during the months when sales are down if your house payment is covered. This in fact can be a useful time to maintain and refurbish your property. There is seldom a shortage of work. Many a professional after sitting all day in an office chooses to increase wealth and security by donning paint-stained garb after work to maintain and repair an investment property. Maintenance can be scheduled around regular work hours like any second job—but it is more flexible.

A multifamily home could also solve problems if it becomes necessary that extended family or a caregiver live close to you, a situation which becomes important as the general population finds themselves caring for elderly parents or retiring themselves, or sometimes doing both at once! You have purchased real estate, whether you use it for added income security or to accommodate relatives or caregivers, whether you are collecting rents or deflecting high costs by housing relatives or trading rent to caregivers, a multifamily home can be your ticket!

Call it a proverbial *Mom and Pop Shop* business, self-employment or just a real estate investment, you can build your investment into a stable home-based business as is applied by people all over the world to supplement income, provide part-time employment and optimize return on investment (ROI) in your primary investment, your home. Your immediate goal may be to live rent-free or at least reduce your mortgage payment but let us not forget the leverage you gain. Well-maintained real estate generally gains in value. Depending on the economic stability in your area your property can double in value in the 20 to 30 years of its mortgage life, sometimes sooner. However, as I said earlier, this is not a *get rich quick* scheme. It may not be as exciting as some investments, but for the long term, it is the best I have found—steady and dependable and quite doable for us average Joe (and Josie) Blows. It is an *equal opportunity employer*—but be warned—you must be diligent and stay on top of things! You make the difference. With good-quality maintenance and competent management, you develop your investment into an income-producing business.

Years of monthly mortgage payments, slowly hacking at the principal and the appreciation gained by normal inflation, will increase your equity wealth slowly but surely. Good maintenance and added improvements can increase these profits hugely.

Plan to spend at least ten hours a month on the financial matters such as collecting and depositing rents, keeping books, staying on top of required licenses, permits and laws, showing properties, signing rental contracts and you will spend additional hours as needed if you wisely decide to do your own maintenance, cleanouts, and repairs.

A dirty apartment after a two- to five-year tenancy can take a couple of weeks to clean when every surface must be scrubbed, painted, refinished, or replaced. As soon as a unit becomes available, determine right away if you need to schedule repairs, outsource carpet cleaning, or replace carpet, and any other needed repairs that may be outsourced. The scheduling will take time so make the calls as soon as possible. Most likely, after a long tenancy, you will need to at least partially paint. I like to outsource carpet cleaning. It is less hassle than hauling around a large carpet machine, especially if you have stairs to climb. Carpet cleaning can be grueling. And the expense is usually reasonable.

Some owners outsource or trade construction and maintenance work; others find it necessary, fulfilling, and even therapeutic to complete it themselves. Although scrubbing and refurbishing a dirty apartment is exhausting, especially when you must paint high walls and elevated ceilings, it provides a great time to take inventory on your current maintenance strategy and plan your next moves. You will also notice small challenges before they become obvious. Over the years I have appreciatively learned a few shortcuts to employ whenever I can. When it comes to walls, the first time you want to paint professionally. After that, where originally it took me three days and five gallons of paint, I learned if I touch up between each tenant, I can get by with one gallon of paint and three hours of work, by spot painting only the soiled, *high traffic* areas in the middle of the walls. No edging around ceilings, windows, and doors.

Overall I do enjoy the therapeutic effect I have felt many times after I have scrubbed cracks and crannies on hands and knees, made all punch list repairs and freshly painted the walls, then sat exhaustedly on the floor among the piled trash and supplies gathered for packing out, in my paint-stained clothes with paint-streaked face and hair, and admired my work feeling a sense of accomplishment, knowing now it will show well and again produce income—but mostly being glad I am finished!

Owning real estate worked for me. I had tried investing in mutual funds, mostly increasing my 401K. The 401k when matched by your employer and has provisions to use for real estate is a good investment and can be your first down payment. Other than that, these methods took money I didn't have. The gains seemingly crawled at a snail's pace and were for the future. I needed to survive the present. If I did manage to hold savings, sooner or later something would happen, and I would need to spend it. Although I would continue to work on increasing my income, my intent was to cut my living expenses in half and thereby quickly increase my disposable income. The Social Security Administration was constantly in the news, where commentators wondered if retirement income would even exist at retirement time. Real estate is a hands-on investment. Values change as the markets cycle, but it is always here, and it is always needed.

Fresh Paint – Cleans It Up!

- Fresh paint - quick and easy cleanup!
  - Outsource for a professional look the first time
    - Consider 3 days labor and 5 gallons of paint for DIYs*
  - Painting between tenants
    - One gallon and three hours labor **
      - Spot paint – no edging around doors, ceilings or floors. You touch up the soiled areas in the middle of the walls.
  - Consider -
    - Outsource carpets cleaning
    - Replace carpet with hard-surface flooring
    - Outsource cleaning between tenants

The Numbers Must Make Sense…

- You must allocate for:
    - Mortgage payments
    - Utilities
    - Maintenance, repairs,
    - Upgrades!
    - Tenant transitions

The California Story

After ten or twelve years or owning multifamily homes, I mentioned to a friend who was considering retirement options that she could possibly supplement her income by investing in a multifamily. She would have loved to decorate them, seemingly enjoyed the light bookkeeping it would entail, was a natural businesswoman who enjoyed people and with her husband's oncoming retirement a part-time stay-at-home job would be welcomed. (It could also solve problems if it becomes necessary that extended family or a caregiver live close to you, a situation which becomes important to some people when caring for an elderly parent or retiring themselves, or in her case doing both at once!) She immediately went into a lengthy horror story about friends of hers who had tried such an adventure. After their tenants abused them, refusing to pay rent timely and after several chances left them with a distressed apartment and loss of several months' rent! They had to resort to legal means to get them out and were barely able to cut their losses and save their own finances.

We may think it strange that they waited till nearly all was lost before they *resorted* to legal means, but this is not so uncommon. People are uncomfortable with legal procedures and don't like to see their names associated with lawsuits; however, these laws are your only protection, and you need to move quickly. *Time is money!* How much you can visualize and how committed you are to succeeding makes the difference.

"You were lucky," she had tossed out at me with a chuckle, thinking she was stating the obvious. Well, maybe it would not work for her after all....

BECOME FAMILIAR WITH YOUR STATE'S LANDLORD-TENANT ACT

Still concerned by her *warning*, I looked up the laws pertaining to the state where I received my initial training, when for a short stint, I had managed a 52-unit apartment complex. According to the Washington State website:

> *"If you are even one day behind in your rent, your landlord can make you move out ('evict' you). If you are behind in rent, your landlord only has to give you* ***three days' notice.*** *… If you pay all the rent you owe within three days after getting the notice, the landlord must accept it and cannot evict you.* ***S/he does not have to accept partial payment.*** *If you do not pay the whole amount within three days, you must move out.*
>
> *"If the rent is not paid within three days, the landlord can go to court and file an eviction process. The process is called 'Unlawful Detainer' in Washington. To start the process, the landlord must deliver to you a 'Summons' and 'Complaint for Unlawful Detainer.' Your landlord should deliver the Summons and Complaint at least seven days before the deadline to submit your Answer."*

A court date may take a week or two depending on the court's schedule and the required time to allow for the tenant's answer. Individual states and even individual judges differ in time allowed after the court appearance for moving out; however, unpaid rent is cause for immediate eviction.

BACKGROUND CHECKS

During my stint as an apartment manager in Washington, I noticed the company we paid to screen applicants, often turned down applicants that I would have approved, mostly because they had no creditor references. This is not uncommon with tenants and is why you rely on the Landlord-Tenant Act laws and always charge a deposit.

Consider a few things like properly screening tenants, requiring credible references, ordering credit reports, and interviewing tenants. Check them out! How long have they been on their job? Have they rented before? Can they give you references? The more lax or vague the state laws, the more intense should be your screening process. And the lower the applicants score on your screening criteria, the more diligent you should be in charging security funds. It goes without saying; a quality, well-kept property attracts quality, well-kept people. However, people have problems, and these will definitely affect you.

Even with the most stringent screening process things can happen that are unprecedented. Screening only glimpses the past. The future is still unseen, and you have to use what information you can get to predict the future. People change as well as the economy, and the rental business realizes many of these changes. Being too conservative can leave you with an *empty* month that can cause you to default on your mortgage. Tenants with past problems that are now required to pay a deposit but are given a chance may have taken steps to secure more dependable employment and never be late again. I find most tenants to be honorable people who are generally responsible and want to keep it that way. Hardships happen for different reasons, and it's frequently people's habits, not their intentions, that give cause for protective laws. Sometimes the economy demands you accept a less-than-perfect tenant.

I find job verification and references to be minimally adequate criteria, as long as I have protected myself by collecting the State-allowed funds, I am protected. Alaska law currently allows first, last and a security deposit equal to one month's rent, plus additional for pets. Even if your tenant breaks a lease or you are forced to evict, your income would be covered for at least a month. You have the last month's rent to cover the month encasing the court actions and the deposit for any other unpaid rent, repairs, and cleanup. With proper precautions, you will not lose as much and in fact may still be returning security deposit funds to them. The entire eviction process usually takes three weeks to a month. If you are prompt, you will still have a few days to refurbish and advertise the apartment before the first of the next month. The first is usually the best time to secure new tenants.

Back to my friends' story: Did these laws even exist at the time when her friends had invested? Probably not all of them, but situations like these are what prompt laws to be written to protect everyone involved and are frequently updated. Landlords and tenants have a definite place in the balance of an economy. State laws protect that balance, but when there is vagueness, you must be more diligent with your application requirements. You must make use of the laws so they can protect you. If the law is written in such a way that it does not protect you, you must protect yourself with security deposits, prepaid rents, and employment confirmations, an intense screening process, and a strong contract. Above all, activate legal procedures immediately when necessary.

THE LAST RESORT

You may use them only as a last resort; however, the *last resort* must be held to a minimum of days. The law demands you must serve notice for a specified number of days and specifies how many days you must wait before you can file to legally remove the tenant from the premises. A proper notice protects both the landlord and the tenant. With a *Seven-Day Notice*, the tenant now has seven *more* days to produce the rent. This may be the break your tenant needs, and it is much better than an eviction, or any other loss of rent. Even when your tenants request arrangements to pay late or split rent payments, write the agreement on these legal forms, using the designated forms whenever possible. Stick to the guidelines. The state's preprinted forms will instruct or include everything you are required to comprise for legal proceedings, should it come to that. Do not wait for the last resort. The legal process cannot be sped up, and remember you are actually being fair to both of you by following the state's guidelines. *The Landlord-Tenant Act* protects and is transparent to both parties.

If it is hard for you to serve a legal notice, you can pay someone else to do it, or possibly leave the notice during the absence of your tenant. If you are uncomfortable delivering a notice, you know the tenant is equally so. It is definitely *the elephant in the room*. Whether they are present or not, be personable. I found it helped to explain the seven-day extension benefits them, such as the additional seven days. Frequently that action stops any further action. People in general do not want to move or go to court and have an eviction on their record, and if they can't pay their rent, it's not going to be a good time to move. Not wanting to be rude or unnecessarily lose good tenants, I added the following paragraph in bold print: ***Your tenancy is valued, and it is understood that you have every intention of paying your rent; however, if you are experiencing a temporary hardship, you must communicate and request acceptable arrangements, immediately. If you deliver your rent to me on or before the end of the SEVEN-DAY period, you may stay, and the tenancy will not be terminated. If a lawsuit is filed and you are evicted, you credit rating may show the missed payment along with the eviction. CALL (xxx) xxx-xxxx. This may adversely affect your credit rating.***

Background checks and credit reports are expensive and time-consuming and may tell you about criminal activities, traffic tickets and even lawsuits, but most of these facts have little to do with whether tenants will pay rent or take care of your property. Employment income and stability verification is paramount. Depending on your demographics, you may want to develop a quick system for background checks. I have found past references to work very well. Granted it could be a tenant's mother you are calling, but even a mother is better than no reference. Yes, it could be that the grown child is so bad Mom just wants to get rid of her—that is why you verify employment and collect a security deposit *and* prepaid rent.

SAMPLE

NOTICE TO TENANT OF TERMINATION OF TENANCY FOR NONPAYMENT OF RENT

To: ______________________
(Tenant)

Re: ______________________
(Address of rental unit)

____
(City, State)

You are notified that you owe rent in the amount of $____________. (This amount does not include any late fees that you may also owe. You may not be evicted for non-payment of late fees.)

If you do not pay this rent by the date stated below (which must be at least SEVEN DAYS after the date and time you receive this notice), your tenancy is terminated and you must move.

Date and time by which rent must be paid: Date: ______________ Time: _________ a.m./p.m.

If you pay your rent in full before this date and time, you do not have to move.

If you do not pay your rent or move by this date and time, a lawsuit may be filed to evict you.

Date: ________________ Signature: ______________________

Print Name: ______________________

Print Title: ______________________

Landlord's Record of Service

Instructions: Serve a copy of this notice on the tenant. Immediately fill out this section to describe how service was accomplished. Complete all statements that apply. Keep the completed original.

□ Tenant acknowledges receipt of this notice on _______ (Date). ______________________ (Tenant's Signature)

□ This notice was personally served on ________________ (Name) by the undersigned on _______ (Date).

□ I attempted to make personal service on the tenant. I knocked on the door, but no one answered. I believed the landlord was absent, so I securely affixed the notice to the entry door of the premises. This was done on the _____ day of __________, 20___ at __________ o'clock a.m./p.m.

□ Tenant was served by registered or certified mail. (I have retained the receipt.)

Date:________ Signature:______________________ Print Name: ______________

Keep a copy of this notice.

After a few evictions in my early years, I began to rely heavily on references rather than background checks. And it worked better than anything I had tried. Quite possibly your applicant could be guilty of all of things listed above but has never been caught or has yet to have a hardship! However, since evictions are public records, you can look clients up yourself and see if they have ever been evicted. Unless it has happened more than once, I probably would not worry, and I do not usually even check—but do charge a deposit. If you are too strict on your requirements, no one will qualify. Instead allow them a chance and protect yourself with a security deposit and last month's prepaid rent if allowed. They get to use their prepaid rent only for the last month's rent, but that relieves them of a great expense at a time when they will have many moving expenses. If they take care of your property, gladly give them their deposit back. The law allows two weeks to refund or provide a written statement as to why you will not refund it. You normally do not have to provide receipts for repairs and expenses. This can be a relief to you if you trade work or complete it yourself. However, the statement must be postmarked within two weeks of their departure.

DEALING WITH PEOPLE

Most of my tenants were responsible citizens who paid rents timely and took reasonably good care of my properties, in both up and down markets. You choose the best tenants you can, but markets change quickly. You can plan for it by timing vacancies, etc., but sometimes you have to take chances and occasionally things go wrong. Tenants have life changes, divorces, lost jobs, etc.

Everyone has hardships—especially young people—which most of your tenants are! Quite possibly a tenant who has been evicted may be more conscientious to ensure it does not happen again, or has graduated to more secure employment so that it will not happen again. Eviction is not a pleasant experience for anyone; however, the stiffer the state laws the more lenient you can afford to be when accepting applications, but you must protect yourself with security deposits, prepaid rents, employment confirmations and either an intense screening process or an interview, or both. I do not know that I am a particularly good judge of character, but most tenants who default on rent, or damage your property do so because of mishaps and bad habits—not bad intentions. Nice folks have problems too. I prefer to look at the facts, verify employment and references, and I find an interview can be quite enlightening and references are usually dependable.

Tenants may be family or friends or become friends but always use a contract and the *Landlord-Tenant Act* law must be the strict guidelines. Do not hesitate to activate the legal proceedings even in a hardship case, or *especially* in a hardship case. A friend or family member who is a tenant may be the hardest to serve legal actions but consider—are you really doing them a favor by being lax? If they are one month late, and you allow them another month—do you really think they can catch up? And by the third month even if they are back to work, it is cheaper for them to rent another place and move. Yours is not the only bill they were late on. Job loss stops everything! Sometimes tenants see you, the landlord, as a rich person sitting on a stack of money, who victimizes poor people by charging too much rent. They don't realize the rent goes towards the mortgage payment and overhead expenses and think it would not hurt you to give them a break, but in most cases their current rent payment is your current mortgage payment. The market dictates how much you could and should charge for your rents.

And sometimes the sincerest people have hardships and are forced to cut their losses. This is not your problem—but do not be a monster. Frequently your tenants will turn out to be the most loyal and compassionate people you have ever known: Paying their rent timely or even early, taking meticulous care of your property, inside and out, getting along with other tenants, and sometimes doing things to maintain or beautify your property at their expense. Usually, it is people's habits, not their intentions, that determine the outcomes. If they do not have one month's rent, they certainly will not have two, and three months can put them over the edge. The *Seven-Day Notice* legally gives them seven more days to produce the rent. That can be a lifesaver in some cases.

On more than one occasion, I have forgiven a partial month's rent for long-term tenants and have even given a free month to a tenant who had lived there three years. On one occasion, a tenant who would get laid off every winter because of the weather, told me he could not pay full rent. Even though he was drawing unemployment compensation. We had struggled through one winter already and now for a couple of months with *Seven-Day* notices and partial payments. Then, standing there defiantly with his arms crossed he told me that he just could not afford to pay in full anymore. After having struggled through the first winter to pay rent with the reduced amount from his employment compensation, he could not do it again.

Exasperated, I asked how he managed to race snow machines all winter. Was that not an expensive sport? He told me that his sponsors supported his racing—even the fuel to travel—and that he and his sons loved doing it and it kept them from returning to an addictive life of using drugs and alcohol. He had shared earlier that he was a recovering alcoholic that no longer partook; however, staying busy to exhaustion with a fun sport was fundamental for his continued recovery. There was no shaking him. He had a surprisingly good situation, and in his mind, he could not afford to change anything. It was all or nothing, he threw the proverbial ball in my court. I am quite sure he knew what a mess I would be left with. He was my largest account; his rent payment was almost enough to make my mortgage payment and I needed it badly. His rent included an apartment and a 1200-square-foot garage that was full of grimy snow machine parts and equipment all covered with engine grime and oily soot—mostly due to repairing and rebuilding

Refurbish Between Tenants

- Vacancy - Renovate and fix minor repairs.
- Never show a dirty apartment
  - Fresh paint – a quick and easy fix.
    - Limited time between tenants
  - Clean carpets
  - Clean and check appliances
  - Check interior plumbing connections
  - Change furnace filters, etc.
  - Charge cleaning and repair costs against security deposits

snow machines—and at any cost I would be left with an expensive mess to clean up—and no income until finished! It's not even a good idea to advertise or show it until it is finished. He did not have anywhere to move it to so most likely he would have to leave much of it there—probably not anything I could sell to recoup my losses, though. The law at the time required that I store it for two months (currently Alaska law reads two weeks) before tossing or selling and besides having to clean it up, I would have to advertise, approve, and accept another tenant in the middle of winter, seldom the best time. Vacancies in the spring and summer are more easily filled. But here in the middle of winter standing on his porch, with neither of us wanting to budge, I could see we both would lose if I proceeded with legal processes and although his hardship was not my responsibility, the cost to me was more than I could afford.

He was standing inside his front door, unkempt and unshaven, wearing clothes he had hastily thrown on to answer the door and he seemingly thought he would be better off if he lost everything rather than give up his sport! We stood politely at an awkward impasse, breathing carefully. He leaned down to pick up a scrap of paper he had dropped, and I took the opportunity to sit down on the stoop. "Look, Gary, I know you can pay part of the rent." He squatted still partially behind the half-opened door, once again on the same level as me, his eyebrow raised. "Your rent is $1750, and you have been here for almost two years. I will accept $1250 a month for the next three months and you can make it up when you get back to work." He broke into a smile and handed over $1250. The partial rent was enough to complete my mortgage payment and although I had required in writing that he pay me off when he returned to work and was prepared to enforce it, imagine my delight when three months later he paid his rent in full and included $1500 to cover the past months' shortages!

He wrote me a thank-you note when he served notice that he would be moving out in two months because of a promotion. The winter was over, and I could more easily rent the apartment; he cleaned it all up and even voluntarily dumped a load of gravel on the driveway. With the oncoming summer employment, I rented it immediately. Sometimes your tenants will appreciate your help and turn out to be the most loyal and compassionate people you have ever known!

TRADING WORK FOR RENT

For a loyal responsible tenant experiencing a hardship, exchanging work for rent and writing subcontracts can be a financial lifesaver for a tenant and in fact can be less harmful to you than evicting, repairing, and re-renting. When an economy is slow, and folks are getting laid off, this can do you both a great service. It is better to lose one month's rent than to lose a month's rent, pay costs for evictions, then spend hours in clean up and repairs, and you are still not through. Now you must advertise and go through the whole process again. All of this is expensive and time-consuming. Time is money. Even though part of your property is sitting empty, you still must make the full mortgage payments. Tenants frequently do not realize, nor is it their concern, that their monthly rent payments make the current month's mortgage payment, and you cannot afford to forgive late rents. If the payments are not made, you will lose your property and tenants will also be evicted. If the tenant is being responsible and trying to cure the back rents, if at all possible, take the high road and help him out. Just remember being compassionate is no excuse for putting yourself in jeopardy! Use the legal processes.

When a tenant gets laid off, he can draw his employment compensation and drink beer all day, or he can cut wood or hitch a snowplow to his pickup and plow snow all winter to supplement the reduced income, or possible take on repair, maintenance, and housekeeping jobs. Many have skills you can employ that will serve you well, creating a win-win situation. Some people are proactive and survive; others complain and see themselves as victims of the system. Frequently an interview with the applicant can be more informative than the rest of the screening process or at least settle a judgment call when the application looks doubtful. One path may result in an eviction process and a filthy apartment to clean and restore; the other may warrant giving a discount on rent if your tenant agrees to plow your parking lot all winter or will perform maintenance or repairs.

Trading Rent or Deposit?

- You cannot evict for unpaid Security Deposit!
- No Deposit – No Incentive
  - It matters when they leave!
  - Habits, not intentions preserve or trash your property.
- Trade rent for cleaning or repair
  - After completed work only
  - Receipts
  - Contract/reduction in rent
  - First months rent for initial cleaning/repairs

Frequently I have prearranged for tenants a discount on rent in exchange for snowplowing or other maintenance. It does not have to cost bookkeeping time either. You give $200 credit every month. If it does not snow much, s/he gets a good deal and if it does snow a lot, it is his most convenient job, and he would probably do it anyway just to get himself out. And what difference does it make to you? You would have to pay it to someone, and a standard amount is more convenient for everyone around, less bookkeeping for both. Go ahead and be empathetic—just be responsible. Being empathetic is no excuse for jeopardizing your investment! Do not even take a chance. Know your limits. Forecast your expenses, monitor your tenants, and play fair.

If your tenant has a genuine hardship, you must decide if you can work with them or if they must leave. You are their landlord, and you are not responsible for their hardship. Having said that, I still encourage you to always take the highroad if possible and work out an agreement beneficial to both of you. If they are taking advantage of you, evict them. A self-proclaimed *victim* can hurt you in more ways than you can imagine.

FAMILY AND FRIENDS

Even when it comes to friends and family, why would you not follow the same procedures as with everyone else? Are you worried about them getting mad at you? They should worry about you getting mad at them for taking advantage of you! You have provided them a home in return for payment. They would have to pay timely rent anywhere they live. You have struggled through the miles to secure your investment. This is your time and money invested, your livelihood, and unfortunately people hurt you, not because of intent, but because of bad habits and practices of which they are probably not even aware. The laws are written to protect everyone involved, respect and use them. Being compassionate is no excuse for being lax or putting your investment in jeopardy!

Always use a contract and charge a security deposit. Alaska law limits the security deposit amount to the amount of the monthly rent, and you can now charge the last month's rent in advance. An additional deposit and/or fees can be charged for pets. All deposits are by nature fully refundable. Charging *a fee* is not always legal and is not really a good practice, either. A deposit is incentive for tenants and security for both parties, whereas a fee is seemingly viewed by many as a prepaid indulgence. Some states do not specify an amount for the security deposit; however, I can tell you it needs to be affordable for the income level of the tenants whom you attract to rent your property, yet enough to cover at least one month's rent in case of eviction, damage, or filth. This is a good time to remember the axiom: *Hope for the best, but be prepared for the worst.* Again, it is their habits, not their intentions and sometimes these characteristics, even with the most diligent screening system are not discovered up front. Sometimes you will have to take your chances and rent to a tenant you are unsure of. Reasonable and fair state laws make it easier and more profitable for you to take your best shot. You must keep it rented! First, last and security deposit equals three months' rent and is sometimes best divided over a couple of months. Requiring a perspective tenant to pay three times the months' rent upfront is often too burdensome and must be split over two or three months, but you will still obtain it. It is paramount that you use a contract and charge a security deposit.

Example of Alaska's Eviction Law

- Jan 1 - Rent due
- Jan 5 - 7-Day Notice (Day 1) non-payment of rent
- Jan 12 - File for court date $180 (Day 7)
- Jan 26 - Tenant is evicted (Writ of Assistance
- Jan 27 - Transfer security deposit
- Jan 27 - Clean and advertise apartment
    - Schedule in advance Carpets, cleaning, repairs, etc.
- Feb 1 - Rent apartment to new tenant.

The Landlord-Tenant Act

Too many people have purchased a multifamily home without learning and understanding the basic laws of their state. Each state has laws that protect both the tenant and the landlord that are not necessarily difficult to understand but do warrant a thorough reading. Usually there is a user-friendly version written for landlords and tenants that can be found on your state website.

Alaska's "*The Landlord-Tenant Act*" includes forms necessary to comply with state legal requirements that you can photocopy, or you can access the state website where the forms can be printed to use. Time is ticking. Your Court's Clerks Office usually provides the forms already assembled complete with instructions, and if the rent or offense is not cured within the noted time, then you must proceed with eviction. The forms themselves cover the crux of the law, at least the parts concerning the specific court action at hand. Many of the forms and regulations are written with the intent to circumvent court action by resolving the issue before it becomes an issue or at least before it goes to court. It is always better to resolve problems without court filings, if possible, but get familiar with these forms and use them without hesitation. For the first step: The *Seven-Day Notice for Non-payment of Rent* should be used immediately to start the process. Whether you politely hand forms to a tenant or affix them to the door, they leave no doubt that you mean business. And, having completed this step, if you are not taken seriously, you have wasted no time in administering the first step. Nothing else can happen until that waiting period, the *Seven-Day Notice for Non-payment of Rent,* is complete. Adhering to and implementing the law will protect you and save your investment. Not promptly activating it could get you into so much trouble you could be upside down and lose everything before you know what has hit you! Research these laws online or ask your real estate broker for a copy of *The Landlord-Tenant Act*. Some real estate brokerages offer classes on *The Landlord-Tenant Act*. These laws are part of the real estate license test, and frequently count towards continuing education in the ensuing years. Your state website will provide all forms necessary to exercise the law. The forms are fill-in-the-blank and are self-explanatory to all parties involved. Legal forms protect all parties fairly and equally.

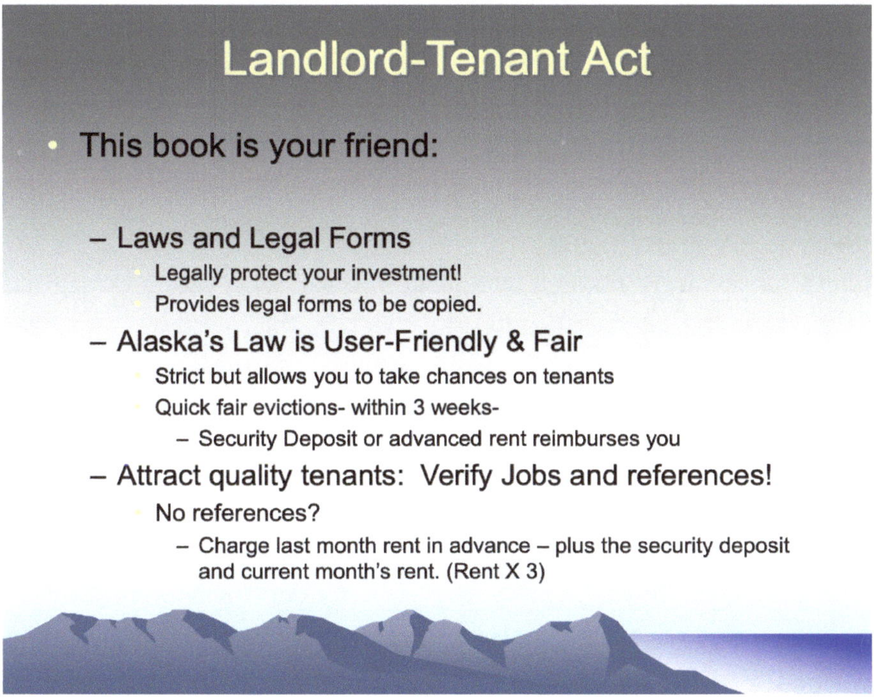

The California Story Continues...

Back to my friend's story .... She had said lucky. *Lucky*? Luck may work well for a while, but I would not count on it. If you can get lucky, it seems you could just as easily get unlucky! This is not a game of chance. Laws and tried and true procedures are actions that have worked for many people, brave enough to venture into the real estate investment market. Having diligently followed the law from the beginning, besides meticulously developing practices for keeping the units rented, after fourteen years I was still surviving. Had her friends known and diligently followed procedures to protect themselves, they most likely could have circumvented their disaster. Many people have done so successfully, but as I said not promptly activating the law could get you into so much trouble you would wish you never started, and yes, you could be upside down and lose everything before you know what has hit you!

SECURITY DEPOSITS

State laws protect, but when there is vagueness, you must be more diligent with your application screening and deposit requirements. There is a reason why they call it a *security* deposit.

Some tenants are chronically late with rent and others have occasional genuine hardships. And even though you do not have to accept partial rent, I strongly advise it, especially if it is not due to continual irresponsibility. Accept it and hand them another *Seven-Day* legal notice for the balance. The more laidback their self-imposed payment timetable, the more promptly you must follow the law. If late payments happen repeatedly or they are uncooperative or avoid you, evict them. Getting your message across at the start may save you hours of work and circumvent the whole eviction process down the road. Collecting rent is your primary focus and can be time-consuming. Did I mention ten hours a month? This can easily multiply exponentially if a tenant is chronically late, and you continue to allow it! When a responsible tenant has a genuine hardship, you may need to write a subcontract to help them catch up, such as the one I wrote for Gary. I have never been burned by negotiating a subcontract for catching up back rent, and I believe if you charge a deposit, adhere to the law promptly and take the highroad when in doubt, you will cultivate loyalty and respect from tenants.

For long-term rentals, I learned the hard way why screening, collecting references and interviewing are important. Some tenants are chronically late and can be highly creative with excuses. One tenant who was chronically late every month would have a different disaster so catastrophic that I could not possibly evict him. One disaster after another: He would get hurt and be unable to work for a week; his truck broke down and he had to spend every penny.... One month he was bitten by a recluse spider and said he nearly died. The hospital had "forced him to pay cash before they would admit him." He showed a nasty wound to prove it. A few times I called him, and he was out in the "middle of the ocean with waves crashing." I am sure he really was—but that is really no excuse for not paying his rent! Your own lienholder is not going to buy it either when you are late on your mortgage payment! His excuses became so creative they were amusing. We struggled through the seven-day notices and partial payments for a few months and finally the struggle was too much. He turned in notice, promising that he would clean it all up if I would refund his security deposit. Always refund the deposit to a deserving tenant—and it usually is cheaper than cleaning it up yourself!

A chronic *victim* can cost you so much time and frequently will unintentionally leave you holding the bag. They do not mean to—it is beyond their control. Remedy: references, interviews, and security deposits.

After one such arrangement, I swore I would never again rent to an applicant with duct tape on his car! All kidding aside the automobile can tell you a lot about a person. Bad credit can be a way of life, and frequently, but not always the car tells a story. I am not talking about an older automobile with mismatched doors or a broken windshield, I am talking about a duct-tape repair. Not only are they ugly, but they are also very inefficient. Some people don't know how to be responsible; I am convinced. I believe the tenant had good intentions but didn't manage his life very well. After renting for a few months, he lost his job, I didn't find out about it until the rent was due again. When I delivered the Seven-Day Eviction Notice, he assured me he had gotten another job. I gave him an extended subcontract to make payments on the back rent. He had so many problems, he couldn't keep the job. The first day he made it to work. The second day, his car broke down on the way. His boss was seemingly understanding about it. The fourth day he was fired. His wife explained: It was the last day for the State-paid medical assistance. He had suffered a cold and thought he might become worse. Since it was the last day of his coverage, he decided to go in as he would not be able to, should his illness take a turn for the worse. He didn't know if he should go or not. The medical office let him come in for the first appointment. Then he went to work. He had called in earlier, but by the time he showed up, they had hired another laborer.

COMPASSION HAS LIMITS

Compassion has its limits. None of us wants to think of ourselves as coldhearted; however, I remember a case where a tenant of a few months lost his business and had to seek employment. He secured employment quickly but had missed a month's rent and now was late with the second month. He could bridge the gap by signing a subcontract I wrote with him to catch up on the back rent, but then things started happening: They had unexpected expenses...the dog required medical care...the wife had incurable medical complications and she explained in detail that the worst part was that although she had paid for many tests, they could not find the cause, but it had become such a problem she had to leave her job. Medical fees were eating them alive! Then he had an accident at work and missed a week. A few weeks later he had a second accident when he fell and broke his arm. It only cost him a day and a half off work, but he happily told me he would get a settlement because he intended to sue them. He had slipped on a wet floor. I had long begun to see this situation as hopeless and now it appeared endless. It seemed that every conversation began with the phrase "more bad news." They stood before me sadly, lips trembling with tears coursing down the wife's cheeks. Resignedly I handed them the final eviction notice, apologizing but refusing to allow more time. They were now over a month behind, and my mortgage payment was overdue. Overdue mortgage payments cost additional interest, a late fee. There is a point where you must cut your losses and act firmly. The next time I saw them, they were in the process of moving and she explained that they had decided to temporally split up and stay with their moms, respectively until they could get back on their feet. I felt honest relief. People have resources they can use in a last resort—not always the kind of situation they want but they will survive. Going down together is not romantic! Compassion has its limits and there is a point where you must cut your losses and act firmly.

Sometimes the sincerest people have had hardships and are forced to change their lives. Perhaps they had illnesses, bankruptcy, or a repossession, and now they must rent. This is where it is black and white. It is not your business to judge them or carry the burden for them. Will they pay their rent timely and take care of your place? Protect yourself but give them the chance. Frequently your tenants will turn out to be the most trustworthy people you have ever known: paying their rent timely or even early, taking meticulous care of your property, inside and out, getting along with other tenants, and sometimes doing extra things to maintain or beautify your property.

Most landlords I know depend on other employment for their main income and use rentals as a supplement. When you occupy your own investment, it is easier to watch over it. Maintenance and repairs are imperative to keep up with as well as updating appliances and periodically overhauling the whole unit. Sometimes jobs or job changes can make this difficult. If your job keeps you away or too busy to keep up with these labors, or you have now moved to another residence (allowed by FHA and VA loans after one year), you may want to trade partial rent to a trusted tenant to manage or to watch over your place and be on call for emergency repairs dispatches. This needs to be someone who gets along very well with everyone, takes exceptionally good care of his own unit and is willing to care for the entire property. Some people do this naturally and can very well be a stay-home parent who is available to dispatch repair professionals in an emergency and can show apartments, assist with contracts, and even collect rents. One four-plex I owned had a large common area between the apartments, where the coin-op washer and dryer was positioned. The apartments were all interior entrances. Things tended to get messy in this area, with everyone taking off their winter boots and coats and setting things down. On one visit, I noticed one of my tenants was sweeping it out. When I commented, she said she had done it for the two years she had lived there but found the other tenants to be non-cooperative. She had health issues and could not work so her funds were limited but she had time. She got along well with the other tenants and seemed to be there for the long term. I immediately offered her a discount on her rent if she would continue cleaning weekly and watching over the other tenants. This gave her authority and confidence to ask others to keep it picked up. The place looked and showed so much better. It worked out great for both of us.

There were a few tough years when the economy was down, and many people were laid off from their jobs. My experience was still limited, and it was a real learning experience! I even had to occasionally depend on my other employment income to supplement the mortgage payments, but it was still a break from paying the whole mortgage myself! I have been through up-and-down markets and have had to learn things by trial and error and so will you but as far as a business in which to invest, I strongly recommend it and would do it all again in a heartbeat!

SAMPLE

NOTICE TO TENANT OF TERMINATION OF TENANCY FOR INTENTIONAL DAMAGE TO DWELLING

To: ______________________ (Tenant) ______________________ (Date)

Re: ______________________ (Address of rental unit)

______________________ (City, State)

You have deliberately inflicted substantial damage (loss, destruction or defacement exceeding $400) to the above premises as follows:

____

____

____

____

Therefore, you are hereby notified that your tenancy is terminated and you must move from the address listed above by the _____ day of __________, 20____ (not less than 24 hours after service of the notice), at _______ o'clock a.m./p.m. If you are not gone by that time, a lawsuit may be filed to evict you.

Signed: ______________________ (Landlord/Property Manager)

Landlord's Record of Service

Instructions: Serve a copy of this notice on the tenant. Immediately fill out this section to describe how service was accomplished. Complete all statements that apply. Keep the completed original.

- □ Tenant acknowledges receipt of this notice on _______ (Date). ______________________ (Tenant's Signature)
- □ This notice was personally served on ________________ (Name) by the undersigned on _______ (Date).
- □ I attempted to make personal service on the tenant. I knocked on the door, but no one answered. I believed the landlord was absent, so I securely affixed the notice to the entry door of the premises. This was done on the _____ day of __________, 20___ at ___________ o'clock a.m./p.m.
- □ Tenant was served by registered or certified mail. (I have retained the receipt.)

Date:_________ Signature:______________________ Print Name: ______________

Keep a copy of this notice.

My First Attempt

The first time I skewered up my ambition, I put my single-family home on the market, intending to use the proceeds to purchase an owner-occupied multifamily in a new area closer to where I worked. I would kill two birds with one stone, so to speak.

As I mentioned earlier, I had done some homework but felt little confidence. That is an understatement. When I think back to how naïve I was, I read a couple of popular "How-To" books about being a landlord and attended a couple of seminars. I took notes and learned great tips I still rely on, but it was always just a little bit unreachable. Like a lot of Americans, I went to work every day, raised a family at night and as a single parent, basically paid bills and skimped on groceries to keep my head above water. I wanted so badly to increase myself, my income, possessions. Mostly I felt overwhelmed. It was always just a little bit out of reach. Research? Where do you even find this fragmented information? The seminars were extremely encouraging but left you not quite ready or wanted additional funds to tell the rest of the story. I couldn't even afford that, let alone a down payment and payments for a property that costs more than two homes when I barely qualified for one! The good news here is that government-structured loans such as FHA and VA loans are written with the first-time homebuyer in mind and allow small down payments, seller-paid closings costs and part of the rental income on the pending purchase can be counted as your qualifying income. We'll get into that more in the chapter on Financing.

Most of what I read made sense, but some things didn't add up. Owning rentals sounded like a great business plan, but how do you get the house in the first place? I read one bestseller where they suggested owning a whole subdivision! They had wonderful day-to-day pointers that I still use today. But buy one at time? That seemed very slow and if you bought a single-family home, and you could rent it for enough to make the payment, but have little left over, what's the point? Sounds like you bought a job that doesn't pay enough! If you have vacancies or repairs, you pay the difference! True, you are building equity but unless you keep up the payments, unless you're the builder, or can refurbish a distressed property and you get a stealer deal on a foreclosure, it just didn't add up.

At this point, I zeroed in on multifamily homes. Not a novel idea, many of us have toyed with the idea of a duplex and supplementing our payment. That part makes sense. But I learned if I stayed within four units limit, I could qualify for an "FHA loan" that would require only a 3.5% down payment. That was encouraging! It made it doable. (VA financing offers a zero-down payment for veterans.)

Still the whole process seemed overwhelming and unfortunately, I am not alone here either. I have been affiliated more than once with young adults who endeavored to buy an investment property. They set out to find an investment as they view each property, not knowing what to look for. Then finally feeling overwhelmed and insecure, they put it on the shelf. They had such great plans, but they were afraid of disaster. All those disasters they imagined really can happen. Investors need confidence and confidence comes through education and experience. Not unreachable but more than your realtor can impart to you in the parking lot of a tenant-occupied property! Not everyone fits the job of property owner/manager. Some owners find it practical to hire a property manager. I have owned investments properties for twenty years, been through up-and-down markets and even had a property burn down! As far as a business to be in, I would do it all again in a heartbeat!

Back to my story, the first time I skewered up my ambition, I put my home on the market, intending to use the proceeds for an owner-occupied multifamily in a new area closer to where I worked. But being between homes, moving my family to a new city and getting the family settled besides working a challenging job is all very unsettling at best and not necessarily the best time to make a life-altering purchase!

My home had sold within a few weeks and with the accepted contract in hand, I had walked boldly into a well-recognized real estate franchise and hired the realtor who was on floor duty. He was very professional and skilled in real estate procedures, but I did not discover till later (and I hadn't even asked), he was not familiar or comfortable with multifamily investments and although he diligently located and scheduled viewings and we tromped through a few homes while disgruntled tenants glared resentfully, he unintentionally disheartened me. Not all realtors are created equal. You want to interview and choose one with experience in the investment field. One simple question, "How many multifamily homes have you helped someone purchase?" and "How many multifamily homes have you or do you own?" can tell you a lot, and the purchasing side is the experience you are looking for. Having listed and sold multifamily homes may be helpful but the buyer truly must beware. You need a realtor with a background in buying them and selling them. Your own research counts highly here also.

My new realtor explained reluctantly that I would have to give a 30-day notice to the tenants to vacate the premises and that the current owners would probably not allow it to be served until the purchase was recorded. The bank underwriter on the other hand would demand that one unit be vacant, so that I could owner-occupy at closing, since I was buying it as owner-occupied FHA. FHA and VA loans allow purchases for owner-occupied only. It is true that underwriters, most likely due to suspicion of fraud, generally will not approve the property as owner-occupied without evidence that one unit is empty at closing. The owners do not want to take a chance vacating a unit because until the documents are signed and the title is recorded in your name, the loan can fall through leaving them with a costly vacant apartment.

At the very least, buying an occupied property would leave me temporarily with nowhere to live. Although I didn't realize at the time that I would receive prorated rents at the time of closing, which would have solved the problem. But juggling a full-time job, having two children in school and a pet, this was not an option. The rental market was good and landlords with available apartments would rent only with a six-month lease. At the time six months seemed like a prolonged time and a waste of my precious money but finding the right property and closing on it can easily take that long! Signing a six-month lease would have been a good choice. Trading one home for another is stressful for the whole family. Finding a property and offering earnest money on a home when yours has not sold creates a contingency that many sellers will not, or cannot accept. Then when it does sell, you have a ticking time bomb, and although *time is of the essence*, the inventory may have changed completely, especially when moving to a different area.

I had not known the right questions to ask when hiring a realtor. Yes, he could identify and show such properties, but were they a good buy? Would they pay for themselves? He was clearly uncomfortable and the few suitable properties available were fully occupied. Of course, I needed to buy owner-occupied to take advantage of the FHA loan regulated for investment properties but that would entail a thirty-day written Notice to Vacate. It was a great market. The economy was good, and it might seem that opportunity was emblazoned like a flashing neon light, but I could not see past the clutter of caveats, one of which was *where would I live while I completed the transition?*

Here was the golden opportunity: a "tight rental market" where no one would rent to me without a six-month lease, prices were up, and some places had waiting lists! All good signs—what a perfect time to jump in! The rental market was great! But being saddled with extra pressures from my job, an approaching deadline on finding a place to move my family, and I was not shrewd about judging the economy. There were so many unknowns, so many things I had not anticipated and always what-ifs.... What if I could not rent it before my first payment was due? Like a lot of people, I panicked imagining problems that in that market could have easily been resolved and the golden opportunity went down the drain.

Meanwhile the clock was ticking. Shopping for homes can be a lot of work! I was so overwhelmed; I lost my nerve and bought a single-family home so I could get settled and get back to work. That was my lesson in why you should interview and find a realtor who specializes in or preferably owns investment property. Ask the right questions. They may be able to educate you or refer you to appropriate places for research. This would be a good test of their knowledge. Any realtor can look on their local MLS and find a listed property. If you are in your first attempt, you may not know all the right questions to ask. Quite possibly they know their stuff or can refer you to a broker or coworker with more experience, whom they can consult. Talk to other successful landlords. Ask the questions and do your research before you sell your own home. When the clock is ticking, you need answers quickly. You need to understand them, and prior research will aid you in asking and receiving proper answers.

Whether a renter or a homeowner you need preliminary information you can find easily. Put yourself in the position of a transitory (homeless) renter and check out the local paper or internet classifieds. Make the calls. Better yet, be a renter. Being a renter is research, itself. I had been a good student to all the popular real estate ads warning about *throwing your money away on rent* and I still believe it, and this would have been a good time to immerse myself in the rental world as a participant, a renter if you will. The experience would have been pure gold to my research. This was a life-changing event, and I needed a lot more confidence. A six-month lease would have been ideal to allow for the searching, researching, and negotiating. And closing papers can be signed near the end of the lease period. If you are a renter or have rented recently, a great part of your research is already behind you.

To invest the proceeds from the sale of my home into a bank certificate to keep it safe for a few months while I rented an apartment much like one, I was looking to buy would have been sensible. (Your credit score will improve here when your mortgage is recorded as paid in full.) You will know how much rent you must pay or charge so you have already researched prices vs. quality, location, availability, etc. A quick check on any realtor's website and a subsequent call to a loan officer would give you an approximate payment. Some websites have built-in calculators so you can do the math.

I wanted so badly to increase my income, my possessions. Always such a daunting task, I felt overwhelmed. It was always just a little bit out of reach.

Research? Where do you even find this unconnected information? The government structured loans such as FHA and VA loans are written with the first-time homebuyer in mind and allow small down payments, seller-paid closing costs and part of the rental income on the pending purchase can be counted as your income! We will get into that more in the chapter on Financing but be heartened there is hope. Nothing is impossible and the information you seek is quite easily found today on the internet on government websites.

Most of what I read made sense, but some things did not add up. They did not always tell the whole story. Owning rentals sounded like a great business plan, don't just buy another job that does not pay enough! If you have vacancies or repairs, you pay the difference out of pocket! True, you are building equity but only if you can keep up the payments. The property must pay for itself. If you are the builder or can refurbish a distressed property and you find stellar deals on foreclosures, single-family homes may be feasible, but for most of us it just doesn't add up.

I was also unbelievably naïve when it came to loans. It is just not the thing we worry about every day and later during my tenure as a loan officer, I found many people share that same uncertainty. The mortgage industry is exciting and well worth taking time to become familiar and although many people are educated or get proactive and educate themselves, for most people it is a once- or twice-in-a-lifetime event. You do your research, select your team, buy your home, get comfortable and get on with life.

But then something happens! The rates drop and your neighbor saves $500 on his house payment *after* he pays off all his credit cards with his built-up equity, and now he is sitting pretty, and you are knee deep in debt. This forces you to research and reevaluate the entire process. This, I believe, is how most people get their real estate and financial education, and believe it or not, it seems to work reasonably well.

Luckily, your mortgage and real estate professionals are standing ready and eager to guide you. Finding a loan officer who will take time to educate you so that you understand the process is fundamental. When you walk into a lender's office with your papers in order and present your case, not only do you feel more confident, but they will also have more confidence in you. The result of being prepared in a fast-paced environment will make a world of difference and it is my intention to bring you to that stage by the end of this book.

Fear

More than once, as a real estate broker, I have shown properties to young adults who had endeavored to buy an investment property. Encouraged by a seminar with a wonderful idea, they unconvincingly set out to find an investment, dragging their backers, usually family, around like dead weights as they view each property. Their deadweight relatives, who did not attend the seminar, murmur on and on, pointing out everything they can find, and finally feeling overwhelmed and insecure the young investors sadly place it on the shelf again as I did for many years before I gained confidence to jump in. They had such great plans, but they were terrified of failure—and rightfully so. All those disasters they envisioned really can happen and have happened many times much like the situation I described above!

Look at the numbers, it's easy math. Will the current income easily surpass the current expenses? And does it allow you some wiggle room if you have a vacant month? One young woman looked interestingly at each apartment, while her parents scowled dubiously. When we got to the last one, her mother pointed out with a grimace the carpet looked bed. Stunned I stared at it. It was only a few months old and was the newest carpet in the whole place, but unbeknownst to me the tenants had overflowed their washing machine the night before, soaking the carpet and although they had tried to dry it out, the dampness made it look discolored and the texture looked somewhat threadbare. Naturally, the buyer and her crew were skeptical of me being the owner and I had already mentioned that the carpet was new. This unfortunately made me look bad—and I was at a loss for an explanation. I assured them that carpets have to be replaced ever five years or so. Later, when I gave her the well records and showed her where I had replaced the pump after my first five years of possession, she panicked and left with a smart remark seriously questioning a property where you may have to replace the pump after only five years. She had no idea how to select a property and her parents, who apparently did not either, had no faith in her at all.

Needless to say, I did not sell it and then decided to take it off the market. That was ten years ago. I have never again replaced that pump—and the carpet? I replace it routinely about every five to eight years. I decided not to move after all and did not sell it. However, I was amazed because it was producing so well and none who I showed it to knew enough to appreciate what they were getting. They viewed me skeptically because I was the owner wanting to sell and although the numbers showed a true picture and the other realtor involved was extremely impressed and told me it was the best deal she had seen in a long time, they didn't believe her either.

What would it matter if you had to spend $500 every five years? Unfortunately, it happens. The property must generate enough income to support that. This one easily did, but I have never had to replace it again. You will always have maintenance and repairs. The discouragement and the overwhelming task at hand apparently were too much but her smart remark had seemingly comforted her parents. I do not know if she ever bought a multifamily home—but she would have been hard pressed to find another one with that ROI. Do the research and do the math. Most of all go with someone who has knowledge of investment properties or go alone. You can always ask for concessions like new carpet and paint in your purchase offer and more importantly you will have time to think it over and even back out before your contract is finalized—even after you sign a Purchase and Sale Agreement contract you still have the inspection and the ensuing negotiations—where you can (even without reason) void the contract. We will talk more about this the next page.

Actual numbers do not always tell everything. Look at the potential rental income and the expenses. If you have done your research, you will know what to look for even without the records. Records may be nonexistent, especially if it is a foreclosure or a new construction or has been under bad management. Actual numbers will not tell you these things. They tell you actual current income and past expenses but do not tell potential and may give no clue as to the skills or quality of past maintenance. Inspect carefully and familiarize yourself with building codes.

I was not alone when I chickened out. As a real estate broker, I worked with the perfect buyer, and he panicked and dropped the transaction. He looked at a very successful triplex. A realtor experienced with multifamily properties, brought him to me. She was excited about it. It was in great shape and fully occupied, pulling good rents. Rates were good and prices were up a bit, but it easily paid for itself. They dubiously checked it out, calling utility companies to verify utilities, asking questions. He viewed and inspected the property a couple of times. He meticulously checked out everything and kept charts. He worked on the North Slope in a two-on-two-off schedule so he liked the idea of living in attached housing so his place would not be left alone while he traveled to work, and during his two weeks down time, he could work on the property. It would fit into his life perfectly. His income was good and although he may have sacrificed space and luxury, the payment was not above a normal house payment. He was so excited! He was approved for financing, and he paid for an inspection, which came out remarkably well. But this was his last chance to escape and for whatever reason he panicked and backed out. His question: What would he do in a down economy if he lost all his tenants?

The economy can give you good hints—if jobs are plentiful and the population is going to work—they will soon need homes. And unfortunately, hints are what you must go by. There is no flashing neon light that says: "Buy this—it's perfect—and the times are perfect!" But seriously, we don't always trust it even if there were.

Turnkey: Slightly Used versus Distressed

Buying a new construction operation that is fully rented and producing income is ideal—but not always available and quite possibly would be priced at the very top of the market. Great if you can qualify to purchase it but keep an eye out for the slightly used. Owners may not be as likely to want to sell when their properties are producing well and the market is hot, even if it is the best time to sell. More frequently owners may have to sell due to financial worries and stresses from other employment. When tenants are plenteous, and the rental market is tight, there will be a reason why it would not rent for the fair market rent, why it would remain vacant while all others are rented. People still need homes—even in a down market. Why is the property vacant? Are the vacancies due to the condition of the premises, the location or bad management? Is there one negative tenant that runs everyone off? Some tenants would rather move than complain about an obnoxious tenant. Is it the location? Check out the surrounding properties. Was there a down economy, a disaster or just bad management? If the prior owner did not keep the property in good repair, good tenants will move and those who remain possibly cannot move—but it will get so much worse—they are not likely to fix it themselves. And if they do not care and you do not respond—if they are still there, they probably feel helpless and hopeless.

Once I helped a client take over a fourplex that was in a great location but was rundown badly. The owner had gotten sick and was bedridden for a few years and then died. No one had collected rents or contacted the tenants, so they continued to live there rent free. They did not purposely tear it up but with no maintenance or response from the owner nature did the job for them. The decks were rotted and had to be removed and replaced. The inside was riddled with water damage. The building itself was about 30 years old but with four or five years of zero maintenance, it went downhill fast. The location, however, was wonderful, and there are loans, notably the FHA 203K, that are set up to rehabilitate such properties; however, it may be easier to obtain owner financing, take out a temporary loan or use credit cards and then refinance once the repairs are made and apartments are rented. Give yourself a time cushion to complete the refinance. Plan ahead. You need to be collecting rents as quickly as individual apartments can be rented to make the current payments. Repairs, maintenance, and upgrades will help support the value.

As an investor you need to evaluate whether you have the skills and funds to undertake such a project. You already know your budget. Do some preliminary research. Check prices and get bids, look up tax records and ask for a CMA (Current Market Analysis), watch the want ads for current rents. Visit similar properties to get comparative values. You may not even consider these, but it can be good information to collect.

MAINTENANCE AND REPAIR

Some people may find management stressful and do not have the stomach for it. Other owners have lifestyle changes where it may become more of a burden than an investment. Rental units, even an owner-occupied fourplex, is a business and must have the necessary time and attention allotted to it. If you start with an older building, you may be surprised how quickly it can go downhill! One leaky pipe or a toilet that "runs" can be the very worst offenders. Keep a watch on shower stalls where continual mold and wetness may cause the sealant to separate from the corners of the tub, and then the shower leaks water down under the tub and down through the floor. Tenants do not always report these or seemingly even notice since it can happen slowly over time. Older buildings are not always properly ventilated, and mold and decay can happen slowly over time, unnoticed by tenants busy with life and unfamiliar with the potential vulnerability. Water-damaged walls can remain unnoticed for years until suddenly the dam breaks and you have an immediate, expensive repair. Unplanned repairs seem to happen at the worst time of year when bad weather strikes and are the most expensive.

A wet, unventilated shower grows mold easily and can be detrimental to sealants and even the surrounds around tubs, and older buildings frequently require new ventilation. Older toilets sometimes "run" unnoticed, faucets drip and plumbing under the sink drips. If tenants have been there over a year, you need to inspect the premises annually for leaks and minor repairs in addition to regular scheduled maintenance.

To Manage or Not

Not everyone fits the job of property owner/manager. Some owners find it practical to hire a property manager, but I do not recommend it, at least not at first. No one cares about your property as much as you do, and property management can be expensive. Losing sleep may very well be what pulls you through your down times and inspires you with ideas to spur you onto success. Your property manager will probably not lose any sleep for you. Many property managers (agencies) are hired to take care of the financial side, collecting rents, and delivering notices. Do not confuse this with building maintenance. Unless you have a specific contract, maintenance will need to be handled separately. Although they can outsource repairs for you, they will probably not take advantage of the option of trading rent for work.

Listening to other owners and reading personal stories can be quite educational with the little things. Robert Kiosaki, author of *Rich Dad, Poor Dad,* revealed one of the most common objections he encountered was that people *don't like to fix plugged toilets in the middle of the night.* "*I don't either*," he quipped, "*I call a plumber!*"

After my first experience with calling a plumber for a tenant, I realized that too is a mistake. Whoever makes the call is responsible for the bill. If it is a structural problem causing the clog, it is your responsibility and the plumber will let you know, otherwise the tenant is most likely responsible. The plumbers will tell you most clogs are caused by flushing too much toilet paper! The expensive overly soft paper advertised for its comfort is *not* good for your septic or pipes!

When sitting through a continuing education class on the Landlord-Tenant Act, I revealed this tidbit and to my astonishment received an admonition that I was "walking a slippery slope" to let the tenants make that call. Apparently even though she had assisted both buyers and sellers in transferring investments properties and was teaching a class on investment properties, she had no experience owning one and had apparently never faced such a problem, but I had been burned already by a tenant who moved out and left me with a bill. The invoice came to me before I had refunded her security deposit, so I was compensated. *The Landlord Tenant Act* allows 14 days to provide a statement of the security deposit, and this is a good reason why. You have time to receive and settle any charges the tenant may have incurred such as repairs and utilities. Who pays for plumbers is not covered in any of the resources I have directed you to; however, it is good common sense. Let the tenants take care of their own toilets. Years ago, as a renter myself, I would never have thought to call the landlord instead of the plumber for a plugged toilet. Had I suspected structural damage, I would have called. Not only can small incidental expenses like that hurt you, but tenants can be abusive. I included it in my contract after that: *You are responsible for your own toilets. Inform me if there is a structural problem.*

Fix Toilets?

- **That's why we have plumbers!**
  - Tenant makes phone call
  - Tenant pays bill

(Ultimately the caller is responsible for the bill.)

Here I will add one more story that justifies telling. I had recently purchased a new fourplex already fully occupied. A tenant complained that her toilet flushed slowly. She had called a plumber and after his visit he explained that it could be the septic system, although the system had been inspected and pumped before the closing the purchase a few months before, I immediately had it pumped again but this did not seem to resolve the problem. When I personally flushed her toilet, it did seem slow, but it did flush. Tenants talk and before long two more of the tenants had the same complaint. The plumber serviced all of them at my expense and since the problem did not go away, he suggested we replace all the toilets. Old toilets do get worn out, he explained with details. He sold me three new toilets and I made appointments with the tenants for installations. My handyman installed the first one which looked much more expensive than the old one. Then he was immediately called away on other pressing business. I did not know that he had only installed one and neither did the tenants since they were not home at the scheduled times, apparently they did not realize theirs had not been installed. When I asked them how the new toilets were working, they all agreed that the problem was resolved. A few weeks later I found the unopened boxes in the shed with what I assumed were the old toilets inside them. When I asked the maintenance man why he had not discarded them, he replied that they were in fact the new ones. He had been called away after the first one and when he got back days later, I had assured him that everybody agreed the problem was gone so he kept the other two but had never installed them. I sold that property a few years later, but toilets were never a problem again. Sometimes toilets flush slowly.

I have owned investments properties for since 2002, been through up and down. I have had to learn things the hard way and so will you but as far as a business in which to invest, I strongly recommend it and would do it all again!

My Second Attempt

Somewhere in between the first and second purchasing attempts, I read *Rich Dad, Poor Dad*, by Robert Kiyosaki, an encouraging book that made it all look doable.

I left my accounting job and stepped into the mortgage world as a loan officer in the late 90s. It was three years before I bought my first property, but I helped a lot of people finance and refinance properties and got a better look at the process. Learning to understand interest rates and loan programs has been significant. Since then, I have become a licensed real estate broker and opened my company where I continued to help people find and purchase properties. And I still find most people are insecure when it comes to investing, properties, loan programs and interest rates.

I bought my first multifamily home, and I kept it for 18 years. Delving into investment properties is definitely a part-time job. This time I had done more homework and was more familiar with typical rents and property values and felt a little more confident than on my first try. The market was in a growth spurt. Investment properties *to purchase* were limited in supply, although rental units were *not* impossible to find *for* rent! Basically, in a good market, people do not want to part with their investments! I understood basic loan programs and how they could work for me. So, watching for a good investment became a full-time pastime. Stay with a newer building, I thought. The few properties on the market were old with leaky pipes, outdated furnaces, leaky windows, and continuous other signs of wear. What about that outdated furnace? Recent building codes had changed considerably, and the newer updated properties seemed a better choice for me.

I understood loan programs and knew I could make them work for me. Watching for a good investment, I knew I wanted to stay with a newer, fully occupied building. Investment properties in general were limited in supply, although rental units actually weren't impossible to find *for* rent! But many of the older buildings after years of mediocre maintenance were looking dilapidated, too much so to wrestle with costly repairs and outdated building codes. The few properties on the market were old and leaky, and smelled musty!

If you have skills and tools, these can be a great choice for you. Count the extent and cost of repair before you make an offer. I was seeing firsthand what happens over a period of twenty years without adequate maintenance. Rental units go downhill quickly without regularly scheduled maintenance, and immediate repairs. If you are not a contractor or handyman, it's a lot more feasible to maintain a property that is in good condition to begin with. Tenants would prefer to rent a clean new apartment even if they pay more. After all these years, I am firmly convinced if your property looks good and is well maintained, you will attract a responsible clientele that will appreciate and take better care of your property.

The property has done well in both up and down markets. Even after years of watching the market, I knew so little when I started. Most people I talk to are in the same boat as I was. We don't even know what there is to know that we don't know! Bravely, we jump in anyway hoping it works. The problem with taking chances is that taking chances can be detrimental! That's where the comfort zone ends, and it is hard to take a step without seeing ahead. I was more careful and luckier this time with the realtor selection. My friend was knowledgeable about investment properties and was able to give me some good tips to get me started.

I like the quote "Hope for the best but make ready for the worst." Do the math. Make the numbers count and trust your judgment.

Acquiring the right investment property was paramount from the first steps of identifying the kind of property that would work for me, obtaining appropriate financing and subsequently owning and cultivating my investment. Investing in properties is not a *get rich quick* scheme but provides security and can prove to be a good investment for future funds, such as college tuition or retirement income. Selecting and buying is only one step. With good maintenance and management, you cultivate your investment to gain in value, while paying for itself and accommodating you. Your immediate goal may be to live free or as close to it as possible, but let's not forget the leverage you gain. Buying a multifamily is a life-changing event and management may be a steep learning curve. When you buy a multifamily, you have bought a business.

As I mentioned earlier, I had done homework and felt more confident, but I still shudder when I think about how naïve I was when I started. Not only had I learned more about the financial end, but my children were older and were more self-sufficient. I was on more stable ground. I had moved back to Alaska, where the economy was growing, always a good sign when investing. I had done my homework and researched investment properties in general. Now I could research the demographical area, and the immediate economy. I didn't want to buy in a down economy. I wanted to start seeing a return on my investment immediately. Like many new landlords, I couldn't afford even one empty month.

I was in a rental unit and looking for a multifamily investment. I read, researched, and questioned those such as realtors, inspectors and builders, people with knowledge. These were helpful, but when I signed on the dotted line, it is somewhat like a starting pistol going off. I was off and running.

IRS Laws and CPAs

The IRS laws allow many encouraging tax benefits such as depreciation to help you cultivate your investment. Unless you are a tax expert, you will want to consult a CPA for more information. In my opinion, tax laws are best left to professionals and other than mere suggestions are beyond the scope of this book. Consult with a CPA, as laws change frequently. One notable fact: I have known more than one tax accountant, attorney or politician who is invested in rental properties. Since they see a lot of numbers and know the tax advantages, it seems a great testament to the integrity of a multifamily purchase. The good news, however, is that the higher education is not required to comply with the business and tax laws. You hire these professionals to advise you. No doubt, multifamily investments will be a big learning curve, as it was for me, but it is doable and my mission in this book, by sharing my story and day-to-day experiences, is to take you through, step by step from your initial interest, through your purchase and well into your successful ownership years.

A very important part of your team is a CPA. I met my current CPA 20 years ago at a Toastmaster's meeting. Frequently professionals and small business owners join local groups for marketing purposes among other reasons. It gave me a chance to interview him. He owned rental properties himself and took the time to explain some things to me. I would do my own rudimentary bookkeeping and the CPA firm basically audited me and filed my taxes. They kept me abreast of changing tax laws and tax advantages. I don't have too much advice about choosing the CPA, except choose someone you feel comfortable with and check them out to make sure they are licensed and in good standing. Their credentials will be displayed in their office and on their website, which will tell you something about their practice.

Check out reviews. Mostly, keep your bank records, credit card statements, and receipts.

From what I understand, the laws regarding income properties are pretty cut and dried. But there are some definite tax advantages with income properties, and that is a good question to ask when choosing someone to help you: What special tax advantages will I qualify for?

Depending on your affinity with tax preparation, there is software you can purchase, or you can even go to a walk-in tax office. If you use your bank account and credit as outlined below, taxes should not really be a problem. I found it comforting to depend on the same professional for the last 20 years.

One piece of advice my realtor, Linda, gave me at my first closing was to open a bank account separate from my personal account and use it only for the rentals. You definitely want to do this—with both your bank account and your credit card. This is 90% of your bookkeeping. All income and all expenses are run through your bank account. Some expenses go through the credit card first, which provides a monthly statement. Save your receipts. If you have to pay in cash, write a check to Self or draw the exact amount and retain the receipt. If you use a bank check, the teller can add a reference note for you. Trades do not need to be recorded since they offset each other. For several years this was my bookkeeping system. Aside from recording my mileage, I would tally up my income, utilities, and expenses, and submit them to my CPA, who was responsible for all the applicable laws and deductions, depreciation, and depletion. It is comforting to me that my taxes are filed correctly and legally.

If you use a software like QuickBooks, all of your books are kept through your bank account activity. My CPA's office set me up with that one years ago when I opened my real estate company, because it was what they used and it would be compatible, but there are a few different software packages that are applicable. A good question for your prospective CPA.

Financing

Now that you have familiarized yourself with the current market, purchasing procedures, and outlined your dreams, you will need to consult with a lender. Here you need some primary information on loans, and interest rates. Keep these in mind as you compile you loan file which I have outlined later in this chapter.

Step 1: Find a lender. Most likely you will be most comfortable at the institution where you bank. I find the larger banks have better rates and fees, the smaller credit unions and brokerages may be much more helpful at helping you put together a package. Especially if you have problems qualifying. You may call a couple of lenders and ask about rates and fees. Everyone has the same interest rates, but margins will differ slightly. A good way to compare is to request a Good Faith Estimate (GFE). You will need this along with an Approval Letter when you are ready to submit an offer. The GFE will tell you approximate costs as well as your prospective payments.

QUALIFYING

Unless you have had a large windfall or sold property, you will probably need to secure financing. Being preapproved and getting all your ducks in a row is paramount to purchasing the correct property. And in a fast market, it can make the difference in whether you get the place you want or not. You will find the property you so carefully researched and finally settled on is the same one everyone else wants and while you are getting preapproved someone else slips in with a contract! Getting your ducks in a row is vital!

Buying your first investment property as a first-time homebuyer is your best option and allows you to take advantage of benefits other loans do not offer. In Alaska, you qualify as a first-time homebuyer if you have not owned a home in at least three years. Alaska Housing Finance Corporation (AHFC) has special rates and programs.

Determining Rents

- What will the market bear? What is fair?
  - CMA – Current Market analysis of rents
  - Will rents collected cover mortgage payment, utilities, repairs, maintenance and your rent?
  - Will rents provide a cushion for unexpected repairs?
  - Can you justifiably raise rents? Add value?
- Established Renters
  - 30 days notice to raise rents (60 is advisable)
  - Consider if problem free tenant with lower rent is better than high rents .
  - Raise rents with transition of new tenants.

*"The **Alaska Housing Finance Corporation** (**AHFC**) exists to ensure that Alaskans have access to safe, affordable, energy-efficient housing. For buyers, for renters...owning a home is more affordable with energy programs. AHFC offers programs that can help reduce your interest rate when buying a home that meets certain energy-efficiency standards or secure a loan for making energy-efficiency improvements to your existing home."*

Mortgage loan programs were created to facilitate and protect the process for the layperson to obtain a home. The FHA does not actually lend you the money; they insure the funds an approved lender loans you; therefore, you must qualify by their guidelines so they will guarantee the loan. Wikipedia.org defines FHA loans:

*"An **FHA insured loan** is a US Federal Housing Administration mortgage-insurance backed mortgage loan which is provided by an FHA-approved lender. FHA insured loans are a type of federal assistance and have historically allowed lower-income Americans to borrow money for the purchase of a home that they would not otherwise be able to afford."*

You qualify for a VA loan if you are a veteran. FHA is the best choice for the rest of us. VA is zero down and FHA is currently 3.5% down payment. They both are beneficial to first-time homebuyers.

FHA, VA, and conventional loans allow up to four units and are required to be owner-occupied, at least for the first year. If you currently own a single-family home, you will probably need to sell it. I usually recommend the fourplex, but a three-plex and even a duplex may suit your purpose. To begin your research, most people will qualify using their combined annual income multiplied by 3 plus 90% of the potential rents x 3. So, if you and your spouse make $80,000 combined gross income and say the rented units produce $1000 each. Multiply the $3000 times 90% ($2700) x 12 months is $32,400 a year. Added to your $80,000 income, that is $112,400 annual income. Multiply this number times three and that is roughly what you will qualify for ($337,200). Your lender will qualify you more exactly, but this will suffice for research purposes. Currently FHA offers competitive rates and only 3.5% down payment. For a $300,000 property that is only $10,500! You will also have closing costs—although sometimes the seller can pay them for you if you ask. If you are eligible for a VA loan—it is possible to buy without spending any money!

Let me pause here to say your real estate, title and lending professionals are your primary connections here and can be worth their weight in gold. Although I will give you the basics and you will be ready to work confidently, they will walk with you through the technicalities unique to every experience. You need to interview them and then once hired, trust them. Do not be afraid to ask questions, in fact question everything, but trust them. This part of the transaction can be a bumpy road. Stay on top of things and work attentively with them. We will talk more about this later, but suffice it to say, you must be able to trust yourself and your own judgment calls. You need to know your limits—without limiting yourself unreasonably. Nobody cares like you do and nobody is affected like you are. You carry the ball here. Your life is the one that goes downhill with a bad investment.

So now that you have identified your potential purchasing ability, what is the actual value to you? What the property is worth to you can be much different than what it is worth to the lender. Besides having it appraised to facilitate the integrity of your purchase, what is the value to you? The lender wants to know if the property is a sound material investment, what is their ROI? And in case you were to default, would they be able to quickly turn over the property and recoup their losses? However, your project must follow a business plan. You already have one in your head if you have gotten this far; however, you need to write it down and outline your income strategy for your benefit. Sketch out a flowchart of the income, expenses, maintenance, and repair allotments, etc.

This is information the lender probably will not even ask for; however, if it is compiled properly, it can be a useful tool for you and the lender. It will be part of the package we will put together later in preparation for your purchase.

FHA AND VA MORTGAGE LOANS

Primarily we will be dealing with two loan types: the FHA and VA mortgage loans. The information below will give you a brief history of how and why these loans came about. These loan guidelines were written to enable middle-class Americans to buy a home, something most of us cannot do without a mortgage contract. Currently both allow up to four units.

According to the official HUD website, www.HUD.gov, FHA operates entirely from its self-generated income.

FHA, Federal Housing Administration, has an interesting history. Started in 1934 by Congress after the nadir of the Great Depression of 1929, FHA made it possible for middle-class Americans to buy a home.

FHA Mortgage

- Funds Required to Close (Example)

• Sale Price	$300,000
• Down PAYMENT = 3.5%	10,500
• Closings Costs (Seller can pay)	10,500
• Funds To Close	$321,000

FHA allows seller to pay closing costs.

*A **VA loan** is a mortgage loan guaranteed by the U.S. Department of Veterans Affairs (VA) for eligible veterans. The original Servicemen's Readjustment Act, passed by Congress in 1944, extended a wide variety of benefits to eligible veterans. VA loans require no down payment and often require the seller to pay costs associated with closing the loan. Since the VA guarantees the loan, you don't have to pay mortgage insurance; however,* *you will pay a funding fee of 3.3% which can be financed in with the loan. VA loans offer many benefits! We won't go into most of them here but if you are eligible, your lender will be happy to outline them for you.*

HINTS ABOUT FHA & VA LOANS

- 3.5% Down Payment
- 75% of Rental Income qualifies as your income
- Owner-occupied for one year
- Only one FHA or VA loan at a time
- Do NOT have to be first-time homebuyer
- One year employment (or proof of training cert)
- One Year clean credit (Can build credit)
- Taxes, hazard insurance and MIP included in mortgage payment
- Interest rates change quickly ... watch them!

Other than the down payment and mortgage insurance requirements, these two loan programs are remarkably similar and allow up to four units, one of which the owner *must intend to occupy* for at least a year. Although you do not have to be a first-time homebuyer, in most cases, you can only have one government-backed loan at a time, and they must be owner-occupied. Both loans have similar limits that vary by region within the state, and from state to state. However, these limits can be quite generous; for example, some areas in Alaska are approved for over $700,000. Both loans require one-year employment (or a proof of training certificate for shorter stints) and one year of clean credit. As mentioned before, your lender can help you build credit. FHA and VA loans rates do not depend on credit scores; however, a conventional loan depends heavily on credit scores.

CHOOSING A LENDER

A good place to start shopping for a lender would be the bank where your accounts are. If you feel comfortable, call a couple of banks, and ask them about their loan programs for multifamily homes. You'll want to ask about loan fees and interest rates; however, interest rates change daily, sometimes multiple times daily, so for now this is not too concerning. Big changes can happen before you are ready to buy.

Your realtor may refer you to a specific bank and/or a specific loan officer, which may be beneficial to you because they can work closely with them, but your realtor and lender can be independent of each other and still work well together. They are your team and will work together to help you complete your purchase. With your permission, they can share your information with each other; however, you need to be confident that they are competent, and you should always be kept in the loop.

Here again, you want someone you can work with, who will take time to explain your course of action. Loan programs, fees and interest rates are not necessarily difficult to understand, but generally they are only done a few times in a lifetime by most people, and programs change periodically. This is the time to get educated, and your chosen lender is here to help you.

With FHA and VA loans, lenders all have the same guidelines, interest rates, and requirements; however, each underwriter may differ slightly, and the institution's fees may differ. We will talk more about this in a future chapter. In the meantime, you need someone who speaks your language. Loan officers and realtors will work diligently to help you close your purchase and neither get paid if you don't! Both professions usually work on commission only, and are frequently extremely busy, depending on the current market. That is why having your papers in order will make life so much easier and can make the difference—if your file is marginal. Sometimes a purchase can come down to a judgment call by the underwriter.

Frequently an investment such as a home or multifamily home is a stretch, especially for the first-time homebuyer. A well-organized application packet can show confidence and competence. This is a file you will construct yourself. Some of it will never be submitted to the *underwriter,* but you will have it at your fingertips, should it be required. You realtor will help you with the Purchase and Sale contract, and your loan officer will help you with your financial file. You will also choose a title company. You may already be familiar with one or your realtor or loan officer will help you. These three individuals compose your team that will work with you through completion of the purchase.

APPLYING FOR THE LOAN - PREAPPROVAL

In the next few pages, I will walk you through preparing a preliminary file to present to the lender. With the packet complete, you should plan on taking a day off from work to meet with your lender. Not only can the application interview take a few hours, but you may need to run around and gather additional items, most of which you would have already had if they had been easy to get. Your completed packet will save you some time here. I have included a list of items below to build this packet.

CREDIT REPORTS

An underwriter wants to know two things: Will you be able to make the payments until the loan is paid off, and can you prove it! Basically, the same things you would ask if you were about to lend a large amount of money to a stranger. The best evidence is past credit history. The first thing your loan officer will do is order your credit history.

Your credit report is a synopsis of your financial life. You and your loan officer will want to check it over carefully even if you think you have perfect credit. You need to make sure all of your credit is reported. Frequently accounts do not get reported if you have never been late or defaulted. These would be your best reports. You definitely want them included! Make sure everything reported actually *does* pertain to you, and only your credit accounts are reported. Reporting agencies get confused with similar names, account numbers, relatives, etc. You may also find your name connected with a spouse or ex-spouse's credit cards if you were a signer on the account or possibly because you were listed as a spouse on the application. These are typically easy to contest and remove. Your loan officer can help you. Even if the mistaken accounts show good credit, they may affect your debt ratio.

Even a report with less-than-stellar credit can often be repaired, although it may take some time if the defaults are recent. Frequently old accounts that were paid off will still show up as open accounts. You may have credit cards that were approved or offered to you that you don't even remember and never used. And since the account is now expired you couldn't use it even if you wanted to. And even though the balance and high credit limit is zero, they still lower your score. Too many open accounts will lower your score. Close them. Merchants are set up to report delinquencies but seldom report the cures. If it was a judgment, it is filed in the court's public records, recruits research court records to glean delinquent information and report them; however, they do not return to check or report if you have cured them.

It is the same with mortgages. When the mortgage is paid off, frequently the reporting stops but is never reported as paid off. This is usually an easy fix.

Too many open accounts can drop your score and hurt you. Your report may show many credit cards that you have never even heard of or may have been closed for different reasons. They may even be preapproved cards that were offered to you. These accounts are obsolete. You can have these removed if never used and reported as closed if it has been a while since you used them. You could not use them if you wanted to. Have them removed. They are harming your credit score.

Although good credit accounts are permanent and stay on your report forever, the good news is that bad credit is subject to the *statutes of limitations* in our legal system and will disappear in time; however, accounts reported as good credit will remain and your score will return to previous highs after the bad credit has dropped off.

If no more negative credit is reported, your score will continue to rise each month if you have a credit record established. Minor offenses such as late payments, parking tickets, bounced checks, and even letting companies check your credit will lower your score, but they will drop off more quickly than late payments on revolving accounts, late installment loan payments or late mortgage payments.

A reported late mortgage payment will probably cost you another year of perfect payments. Mortgage underwriters do not like to see late mortgage payments and loan guidelines usually require you to wait one year after a late mortgage payment is reported. You can try writing a letter if you have a good excuse, but it is probably better to deal directly with the mortgage company that reported it. If they will not take it off, you had better have a good explanation complete with proof even after the year is over. Most likely you will have to wait the allotted time before applying; however, keep any letters you have written or received and/or notes from phone calls to accompany the letter of explanation (LOX) you will write to the underwriter. You will still need to explain this even if it has been a few years. Even a bad explanation is better than none. Sometimes "*We screwed up…*" can go a long way.

Foreclosures and repossessions are the worst culprits and stay on your report the longest—even longer than bankruptcies and they can hurt you worse! One theory is that as detrimental as a bankruptcy is, at least you have shown some responsibility to settle debts, where a foreclosure or repossession shows lack of caring. Not necessarily true—but that is the belief.

By the way, if you have filed a bankruptcy, you must wait two years to be eligible for FHA or VA loans and four years for conventional loans.

A repossession or foreclosure usually takes the full seven years or longer to clear and suggests that you did not try to resolve it. Although you do not necessarily have to wait the whole seven years you will need to write a letter explaining it. The underwriter wants to see that you have taken steps to make certain it will not happen again. Here is where a well-written letter to the underwriter can help you if it does in fact still show on your report. Bankruptcies and foreclosures can stay on your report for ten years even. If you have reestablished your credit and paid all bills and expenses on time, the letter will carry more weight. Include all the documentation you can retrieve proving or explaining the cause, medical causes, lost job, etc. Here again sometimes the best letter says, "*We screwed up....*"

So, check your credit and if possible, repair it. This may cost a nominal fee, and sometimes it may be wise to hire a company that specializes in cleaning up credit history. This is usually a more significant fee. The best way to build good credit is to adhere to a budget and pay all bills on time.

BUILDING CREDIT AND ESTABLISHING CREDIBILITY OF FUNDS

Absence of bad credit is wonderful, but frequently first-time homebuyers have not *established* credit at all, or it has been a long time, so scores come back as zero. The credit bureaus have never heard of you. Establishing credit is a process that you can and should start immediately. High credit scores are what they want to see, but with FHA, and VA loans, you may need to *build* credit.

If you have paid bills, even rent and utilities, and you can prove it, your loan officer can help you establish credit through the bureaus. If you split rent with someone, is your name on the contract or can you show cancelled checks or receipts to prove you paid? And timely?

If you did not have your name of the rent agreement, or the funds came from the roommate's checks, will your landlord give you a statement verifying that you have paid timely? If you paid or shared utility bills, is your name on the accounts? Add them officially as quickly as you can—even a record of three months is better than none. Usually, your loan officer can submit these to the credit bureau for you.

Utility companies make good references. Receipts, receipts, receipts! Provide records or letters with contact information for past landlords or other creditors or better yet, request a letter from them showing your record and including their contact information. It may be quicker to write the letters yourself and ask them to sign it, thereby ensuring it gets completed and they verify all the information you need: dates, amounts and contact information.

Bank statements are an excellent record to prove payment history, and loan guidelines generally require that you own a bank account. Your bank statement can also tell the underwriter a lot about you. You never want to turn in a bank statement showing overdrafts. They also show a lot about how you manage your money. Does the money hang around for a while or does it sweep through your account draining it every month? Not so bad if there are no overdrafts, but it looks much better if the balance stays above zero at the end of the month.

If you have no past rent or utility payments and paid cash for your car there is still hope. There is no time like the present to start building a credit history.

A well-rounded credit report will include a mortgage or rental history, an installment loan and two revolving lines of credit. Underwriting guidelines call for four lines of credit to have been reported; however, they do not all have to be active. They can be recent past credit accounts.

An installment loan is one where you buy something on credit and make incremental payments until it is paid off such as a loan for an automobile or a refrigerator. Revolving credit is a credit card or account set up so that you may use it again and again even while you are paying for it.

Obtain a credit card for the purpose of building credit—even a prepaid card, use it once and then pay it down, without charging again. As your balance lowers your score rises, the same with all reported credit. Paying down on your balances is one of the best ways to raise your credit score. The report shows your highest credit amount and how much you have paid. This difference bodes well on your credit score. Frequently the home purchase is a squeeze for the first-time homebuyer (FTHB); suffice it to say, the higher your credit scores the better. At any rate, creating and maintaining a good credit report will open a lot of doors currently and down the road. Start early and protect it.

Most lenders require that you have a bank account. This is occasionally waived for some segments of society like immigrants who do not trust banks and habitually keep cash. I believe the rule is that it must be a *common and accepted way of life* for their culture, and it is referred to as *mattress money*. Mattress money is untraceable, and lenders will not consider it in most cases. Yes, that is absolutely true! If it has been in the bank for less than two months, you will have to prove a credible source for money that is not *seasoned* and does not appear to be from wages or other obvious sources. If it has been on deposit for more than two months, it is considered seasoned, and you do not have to explain it. Any larger-than-normal deposits on your current bank statements must be explained with proof, most likely to ensure they are not a loan (which would increase your debt ratio).

Note: FHA loans do allow gifted funds for your down payment. These funds must be from a party with vested interest, i.e., family, spouse, etc. This will require a gift letter that specifies it is a gift and that you will not be required to pay it back.

THE NEXT STEP STILL IN LOANS

At this point, the mortgage originator can usually tell you if you qualify to proceed. If scores meet the minimal requirements, you have passed only the first step. Now you must prove your income and job stability.

During my tenure as a loan officer, working closely with first-time homebuyers, it became increasingly clear that most people do not keep good personal financial records. Whether you set up an elaborate filing system or throw unopened bank statements into a drawer, it is imperative that you keep your bank statements, as well as your paystubs. Somewhere in that drawer you need to include those extra copies of your W-2s. Forget about setting up an elaborate system, just keep these in an easily accessible place.

Assemble your loan application package and keep it up to date. The following list will get you started:

- 1 month's paystubs (or two consecutive months' if paid monthly)
- 2 years' W2s or taxes if you are self-employed
- 3 months' bank statements
- Proof of any other qualifying income
- LOX – Letters of Explanation for delinquent credit or job gap histories
- PFD – Permanent Fund Distribution or other dividend distributions. In Alaska you can count the PFDs of your dependents.
- If you have filed bankruptcy within the past few years, you will need to include copies of your legal papers.
- If you are self-employed or have other income, you will need copies of your taxes instead of W-2s.
- If you have been recently divorced, receive, or pay child support, you will need your legal papers. If you pay child support, it will count against your debt ratio. If you receive it, it qualifies as income.

- If you recently sold a home, you may need to produce the HUD1 statement (the final settlement recording document) as these may not have yet been reported.
- For credit problems or employment gaps, you will need to write letters of explanation. These do not have to be elaborate, just be honest. You are certainly not the first credit offender. Some people have medical disasters, coupled with loss of incomes, or divorce stories when one spouse went berserk, lived on credit cards for a few months and destroyed the joint credit. Interestingly enough, both ex-spouses frequently use this same story. Apparently "exes" are notoriously bad credit risks.
  - Frequently young adults are bombarded by preapproved credit card offers before they even graduate from high school! Inexperienced uses of credit and job losses are credible reasons for credit blights. Believe it or not, underwriters are people too and they do understand this. It is not unreasonably to believe they may have been in any of these situations themselves.
  - You want to foresee and explain every possible past predicament such as credit blips, employment gaps, etc. Write these letters ahead of time. Explain each dilemma briefly but truthfully and have them ready. These may be simple explanations and they may require additional documentation to prove them. Have them ready ahead of time, complete with documentation necessary for proof. You may not need them, but your loan officer can decide if you do or not. Usually, you do.
  - The underwriter wants to know if you have cured your mishaps and what you have done to keep them for recurring. If you have a spotty job history, what have you done to ensure continued employment? Job experience is golden but a month here and there of unemployment can be enough

to put you in foreclosure. A short-term layoff and a projected return date usually ensure you can draw unemployment compensation, which will hopefully bridge the gap. If it happens every winter, you may still be okay. Some jobs are seasonal and short unemployment periods happen cyclically. The underwriter can consider it *usual and customary*, and all your income is averaged for the year.

- You are required to show one-year continuous employment. If you have changed jobs, it must be the same type of employment. If you have changed to a different type of work, you will want to provide some proof of training or schooling. Workshops or classes, even one-day training certificates will go a long way to show you have taken responsibility and will sometimes enable the underwriter to waive the *one-year continuous like-employment* requirement!

Applying for Your Mortgage

- 1 month's paystubs
- 2 years W-2s
- 3 month's banks statements
- Assets: 401(K), retirement account, etc
- Recent divorce settlement
- Recent bankruptcy papers (2 years)

- Other proof of income
- LOX – Letter of Explanation (credit history and/or job gaps)

PAYMENT SHOCK, SECOND JOBS, AND OVERTIME

Payment shock is a term mortgage professional's use to describe a large increase in mortgage payment. For example: Your new mortgage payment will be $1750 but you currently pay $1250 for rent. Can you produce evidence to show that you can make the higher payment? Either you or your spouse must document increased income or provide documents showing you have recently paid off an obligation, or consolidated small loans, credit cards, etc., into a larger loan which requires a lower payment.

If, however, you have made regular deposits into a savings account, 401(k), etc., close to the amount of the funds you'll now be using for your new payment, i.e. $500 a month, even though this is probably at least part of your closing funds, this payment shock malady can be waived, but unless you can evidence this, the underwriter will probably not believe that you can cut back your general living expenses if you have no way to show it. Even if you swear it is because you are used to eating expensive pizzas every evening, the underwriter will not believe you will stop after closing. Habits do not generally change that quickly. LOL. You need to stop now and put the money in your bank account for a few months.

While it is true that you can cut back on necessities for a while, sooner or later it will all catch with you. People can or will only suffer for a while. If you are unemployed for a while, you can make do. Then you get hired and get a paycheck: a beautiful large paycheck. Kiss it quickly because it will hit your bank account, diffuse seemingly into thin air and be gone immediately. Even if you have kept up on your bills, now your supplies are used up, clothes are worn out, or outgrown and you must replenish everything. You can do without for a while, but sooner or later you must catch up. If it is a matter of cutting down on pizzas and eating homecooked meals or carrying a lunch instead of eating out, a good strict budget will come in handy, but start doing it ahead of time and deposit the saved funds in a savings account. You may save more than you think. Only one latte a day can add up to over $2000 a year, and a fresh pack of brand-name cigarettes is twice that much!

Years ago, before I purchased my first home, I made a game out of saving money. I bought cans of *Van Camp's Pork and Beans*, which were three for $1. Then I bought freshly ground peanut butter and bread from the local *Nature's Market* each week. Between those two items I covered the whole week's lunches and spent about $6. I have to say it got old pretty fast—by the time my house closed I was ready for a change in diet.

Income from a second job is judged on the same principle. Most people can only continue two jobs for a short while. But if you can show that you have continued for two years—even seasonal employment—the underwriter can accept it.

Overtime also works with this principle. If it is usual and customary or has continued for two years, they will allow it. *Usual and customary* are the key words here. Many workers receive overtime on a continual basis and if in fact working overtime is required, it is considered usual and customary even for shorter periods.

Your loan officer or originator may very well give you an additional list of documents you need to provide. The above list contains the basic needs, but each case is different, and you need to supply these documents immediately. Your loan does not progress without them. The more complete your package is the less time it all takes. Loan officers, processors and underwriters love people who come in with it all together! When you walk in with your documents in a pile, they will love you. They will do the work, even filling out your application; just supply the necessary documents as quickly as possible.

Do not call and ask how your loan is coming along. If they are waiting on documents, they are waiting, and nothing happens until they get them.

APPROVAL LETTER AND GOOD FAITH ESTIMATE

When you have been preapproved for a purchase, your loan officer will give you an approval letter (sometimes referred to in Alaska as a 90% letter) and a Good Faith Estimate (GFE). Both will show the amount for which you qualified for, your prospective loan costs, the potential interest rate and potential mortgage payments which will include principal, interest, taxes, and hazard insurance (PITI). Your rate will not be locked until you have contracted a property. The GFE will also show mortgage insurance premium.

HAZARD INSURANCE VS. MORTGAGE INSURANCE (YOU WILL PAY THEM BOTH)

Hazard insurance or *fire insurance* insures your home against loss. It protects both you and your lender.

Mortgage insurance protects the lender in case you default on your payments: If you bought a home for $100,000 and put a down payment of $20,000, you would own twenty-percent equity. The lender or lienholder owns eighty-percent equity.

$100,000	
($20,000)	Your equity
$80,000	Lender's equity

If you were to default on your mortgage, the lienholder most likely could sell your home for at least eighty percent of its value, or $80,000 and since you have already paid twenty percent, or $20,000, they would suffer no loss. You, however, would lose your equity of $20,000.

If the property is damaged or the economy has declined or for whatever reason it will not sell for enough to pay off the balance owed ($80,000), the mortgage insurance will pay your lender the difference. Mortgage insurance protects only your lender, not you. If you default, you lose the property and your down payment funds.

You pay the mortgage insurance, but it protects the lender. With FHA loans, you are paying only 3.5% of the appraised value for your down payment. FHA and VA loans do not allow you to pay more than the appraised value. Your lender now carries the mortgage at 96.5% of the appraised value. Assuming if you defaulted, they could still make a quick sale for 80% of the value, they would lose 16.5%. Mortgage insurance pays them that difference, so they do not lose any funds. You, however, will lose the property and the 3.5% and any other funds you have invested.

As you gain more equity over the next few years, the lender's risk diminishes; ideally you owe less than the current market value. After a prescribed number of years, the mortgage insurance falls off or when your equity reaches 20%. If your property appreciates in value due to the economy, you may apply to have it removed sooner than this. This usually costs you the price of an appraisal, but sometimes they will do a *Streamline* and not require one.

According to the official HUD website, www.HUD.gov:

Currently FHA allows up to 90% LTV (loan-to-value) before mortgage insurance, better known as MIP (mortgage insurance premium) is charged at 3.5%. You will pay 1.75% upfront, financed in with your loan and the remaining 1.75% is included in your payment for the next eleven years, unless you pay the loan off earlier.

DEBT-TO-INCOME RATIO

By analyzing your financial portrait your loan officer will determine your debt-to-income ratio. Referred to as your DTI, it determines what percentage of your monthly income will be allocated to mortgage payments, and what percentage is already being spent on other obligations. What is left over for payments?

A perfect FHA loan will have a DTI of 28/36. This allows that almost a third (28%) of your gross income will be paid to a mortgage company, and additional eight percent (28 + 8 = 36%) is allowed for all other obligated payments, the type of which are reported on your credit report, while a VA loan allows 41% on the back ratio. These guidelines hold that the remaining 59-64% of your income is used for general living expenses, tax withholdings and voluntary deductions which are not considered. Depending on the *strength* of your file, these ratios may be expanded if the underwriter sees evidence of stability and/or higher income potential, and this is where a higher credit score and well-written *letters of explanation* (LOX) can help you.

RESERVES

What are reserves and why are they important? Reserves are reserved funds you have socked away for a rainy day, retirement, etc. They are necessary to protect you in case of disaster. Reserves show the underwriter that you have sufficient funds reserved for such incidences. They also indicate responsibility.

An ideal applicant will have a long-term stable job, clean credit with a credit score above 620. Besides owning reserves such as a 401(k) or other retirement or savings account, etc., you must fit within the DTI guidelines. Unfortunately, not all of us have stellar credit or job experience and a 401(k) may be only a pipe dream.

Reserves can go a long way toward loan approval if you are weak in other areas of your file such as job stability or minimal credit. If you are strong in other areas of your file, these are sometimes waived. Again, all funds must be seasoned or justified.

This sounds like a lot of money which most of us do not have sitting around. Please do not get discouraged yet, this is a big hurdle and as I have said, owning a multifamily can give you the stability you need to increase your disposable income by supplementing your largest monthly disbursement. If done diligently, it can gradually increase your credit score and your power and give you freedom to spend your job-generated income on things you want.

As I said before, investing in a multifamily can be surprisingly inexpensive to get started, and can return profits immediately. In fact, if the property is fully rented, you will begin collecting rents one or two months before your first payment is due! If the purchase is closed at the end of the month, the payment will not be due for at least one month—but you collected rents the first month and will collect again the second month—so you will have collected two months' rents when the payment is due! If the purchase closes mid-month, you get prorated rents and possibly collect the next two months' rents before your first payment is due. These funds are not reserves, but they may be a good thing to point out the Underwriter and can be kept as such.

Finding the Property

Older buildings, suffering from lack of building codes and maintenance, looking dilapidated, with costly repairs and updates to building codes, are way too much so to wrestle with. If you have skills, tools, experience, and knowledge, these can be a great choice for you. Skills and tools are always a plus, even around your own home, and every time you clean and refurbish an apartment you will find minor things to tighten, shore up or remove but consider: How deep do you want to get in? How much work can you afford to buy?

At any rate, I was seeing firsthand what happens over a period of twenty years without adequate maintenance. Rental units will go downhill quickly without regularly scheduled maintenance, and immediate repairs. If you are not a contractor or skilled handyman with tools, it is a lot more feasible to maintain a property that is in good condition to begin with.

When my friend, an accomplished realtor, familiar with the area and had dabbled in investment properties herself, called and told me excitedly that she had found one, and it was "the best one she'd seen in a long time," I checked it out and did the potential math. It would work for me. The market was pretty much at its peak and listed at the top-of-the-market price, which I paid. That is a story too! It was new construction, fully rented and drew enough income that it would easily pay for itself. It had potential for additional rents and income. I saw possibilities galore; however, the appraiser did not! He appraised by the GLA (general living area), aka square footage of the building, not the potential income. Back to the negotiating table again. We were able to renegotiate a few dollars —but I would have paid the price if I could have secured the financing. Checking the numbers and doing the math is fundamental, but *seeing* possibilities is stellar! Is it the kind of place you would rent for your own family? Is the maintenance in line with your skills and time constraints? Are there possibilities to expand your income? There seemed no other choice and this is one property I kept for eighteen years because of the possibilities I have been able to expand.

The immediate surprise was that at closing, the current rents were prorated and turned over to me. Since we closed of the 15th of the month, one-half of the rents for that month were prorated and paid to me. We closed September 15th and the first payment was due on November 1, so I also collected October rents and November rents before making the first payment on November 1. And just like, after my first payment was made and with $5 grand in my pocket, I was off and running as an investment property owner!

Funds You Receive at Closing

Close 15th of September

Example:

OWNER OCCUPIED APARTMENT

Rent X 3 units = $3000/month

• Prorated rents	= $1500
• October rents	= $3000
• November rents	= $3000
SUBTOTAL	$7500
• Mortgage payment	=($2000)
• Utilities x 2 months	=($500)
BALANCE	$5000

Example

You could say I was luckier this time with the realtor selection. My friend was knowledgeable about investment properties and could give me some good tips to get me started. She introduced me to *The Landlord-Tenant Act*. I did not even realize how much help she had been. When I think back to my first attempt in the 90s, I cannot help but wonder what kind of disaster I might have gotten myself into seeing how uncomfortable the realtor was with the whole situation, he probably wouldn't have been any help at all! Shopping, writing an offer, following through to closing and recording of the title only put you at the starting line. Now you are off and running and you need to trust your real estate licensee, and your title officer. The lender for now is out of the picture and the limited help available from these two is all you have. Time is of the essence now and experience is pure gold.

It is the unknowns you need to learn about, and economies fluctuate so even a few months can make a difference. What are comparable units renting for? Which options are being offered? Who are your most likely tenants? Will you be able to lower your rents, if necessary, to squeeze through a bad economy? These questions when considering neighborhoods and kinds of properties are important. Look at diverse properties and ask questions to the owner or manager. Sometimes they will share valuable information with you. If all the prices seem high, but suitable properties are in short supply, it is a good time to jump in but how long has this continued? Know that the economy will again cycle down. All these things you have previously studied now come to the foreground. Make hay while the sun shines but like a squirrel store away for the winter.

Beware of the "top-of-the-market syndrome" where investment properties become so popular, and prices become so inflated that you pay the highest price right before the economy cycles down. Predicting the economy is complicated even for scholarly economists and learned investors, but it is not necessarily a bad time to buy. Be assured it will cycle down and we need to take it to heart and protect ourselves.

What are the current rents compared to the availability of rentals? What happens when jobs are scarce, and rentals are plentiful? This is where the rubber meets the road, and you need to be prepared. It is not impossible. People always need homes even in a down economy. What can you do to make your units more desirable? What will keep your units rented when there are vacancies galore?

Unless it is a major recession and the town shuts down, even in a slow economy, people need homes. A good solid investment will transcend the cycles of the economy. You may need to adjust your rents or supplement the payment yourself. Will you be able to afford to? Always continue with the routine maintenance, trading it for rent, if necessary, but improvements or remodels may have to wait till the economy recovers. If you have kept up on maintenance, it will not hurt you. Units should be refurbished between every tenant, but extensive refurbishments should be routinely completed every few years. Keeping your property in top shape is paramount. And even broke tenants take better care of places that are well kept.

Assuming, since you qualified for your purchase with your full-time job, you want to find a newer building in good condition that does not need work, and then have it inspected and repaired before you take title. Even for an experienced repairperson, repairs take time. With a fulltime job that may be a problem. There is only so much of you, and you will have plenty of maintenance and upkeep soon enough. It is an ongoing process. Sometimes trading maintenance and repairs for rents owed works out good for both you and your tenant. Many tenants are blue-collar workers, and they frequently have useful skills you can utilize without paying the overhead you would pay to a commercial business.

Preferring to do most of my own cleaning and refurbishing, I have developed beneficial shortcuts, although I outsource plenty. I repaint walls and polish the entire interior but usually outsource carpet cleaning and replacement, as well as plumbing and electrical repairs. I have seen the paramount importance of quickly and completely refurbishing every apartment every time it changes occupants, performing routine maintenance, and inspecting for damages such as unreported leaks or damaged appliances. Depending on my workload, sometimes cleaning is outsourced.

Over the years I have learned a few shortcuts. Where painting an apartment used to take me three days and five gallons of paint, now it takes one gallon of paint and three hours, to have a freshly painted apartment ready to show. Time is money and work makes you very tired—whenever you can save on either, you win. Write a simple contract and assign dollar amounts to be credited against rent if you hire your tenants. Many tenants suffer because of job layoffs. If you have maintenance work to catch up on, blue-collar tenants are often in the same businesses that you would hire anyway and crediting their rent helps you both out. A word to the wise...the work must be completed before the credit is given. I bet you have already guessed why!

When You Have Identified a Property

With your approval letter and GFE in hand, you will meet with your realtor. Even if you have consulted a realtor and even searched for property, most realtors will not invest too much time until you are preapproved for a loan. Now you are ready to go. These preceding steps are important because in a hot market, any property you love will be loved by everyone else too. And when you see potential, so do they. You will find you may have some very stiff competition. But now you are in the position to move in and snap it up! By the way, you will need to keep your loan file updated. If you take more than one month selecting and negotiating for your property, you will need to produce your next paystub and bank statement.

Let us stop here and recapitulate:

- You have researched what kind of property you want to find.
- You have verified, established, or cleaned up your credit.
- You have provided everything required for preapproval.
- You have your approval letter and GFE (Good Faith Estimate) in hand.

Now you are ready to go…no holds barred! So here we go. Hang on…it is about to get bumpy.

You do not necessarily need to use a realtor, but it will be money well spent. Usually, the seller pays both realtors, which was arranged when the property was listed. Hopefully, your search will not take forever but it can easily stretch into months, even when you are actively looking, depending on the market. The problem, I found, with a good rental market is that there are few multifamily properties for sale. In a down market many properties are for sale but are missing tenants. Be ready and persevere. You will find one and you will recognize it because you will know how to read the numbers.

Distraught and foreclosed properties may be eligible for an *FHA 203K loan* which is a rehabilitation loan. Most lenders do not want to bother with them because they are time-consuming and troublesome. Short-term owner-financing may be a good alternative here. Once the repairs are complete, the property can be refinanced through a bank and the owner paid off. Besides all the documents you have already compiled, you will want to add a resume. The lender needs to be convinced that you will not make a big mess and leave them with it. So, make it a good one. If you have enough construction experience to complete a renovation project, make up a folder of building plans, materials costs, and labor hours. You will want to include photos of projects and jobs you have completed, with references. If you do not have enough experience, make a list of subcontractors, complete with their bids. These loans are hard to work and unless a particular lender specializes in them, you may want to go a different route, such as owner-finance until the property itself qualifies for a loan. After a period of making timely payments and if possible, collecting rents, your credit and equity will improve.

For now, let's say you found a property in good condition that is at least partially occupied. Before you make an offer, ask your realtor to create a current market analysis referred to as a CMA. Your lender will order a formal appraisal before you close the loan. The appraisal is for the underwriter and although it may show current rental rates, the income is not considered in the appraised value of the property. The rents do, however, apply to your debt ratio, and the appraisal may be used to confirm them. The appraisal is for the value of the actual building and land. The projected income you anticipate is from the *business* you run *within* the building. With FHA and VA loans the property must appraise for at least the purchase price. FHA and VA guidelines do not permit the buyer to pay more than the appraised value or to purchase a substandard property.

Your realtor can provide a CMA (Current Market Analysis). The CMA will give you a ballpark picture of what it will probably appraise for and what your offer should be. Trust your realtor here. He may not know any more than you, but if you are on the same page, he has information at his fingertips and can research it. Don't be afraid to ask questions. As a loan officer and later a real estate broker myself, I have seen people offer too low and lose out on their dream property, only to settle for another property and pay more for less value. Trust your realtor here to do the job for which you hired them. The market changes quickly and often and people who work with it daily are closely attuned to it. Many times, clients seem stuck because of a bad experience or a disastrous news story. Some were terrified of various types of loans, such as *variable rate mortgages,* because of bad happenstances. Markets change. Many sellers ask for a CMA before they list their property. Others use different methods of assigning prices, and they vary as widely as the sellers themselves. Some properties will be priced at pie-in-the-sky, while others may be priced more appropriately. It is important to know the difference. Trust your realtor to help you here. You need to see a CMA for the value of the building and another for the rents it earns. You need to research the debt ratio for the property itself, i.e., payment vs. rental income. Your realtor will ask for the owner's taxes later to show the expenses, but sometimes you can preemptively research the utilities by calling the utility companies directly. Utilities are a big expense and can vary greatly from place to place. These are your basics on which you will base your offer.

Your lender will order an appraisal before your loan closes after you personally are approved, to assess if the property will qualify; however, your realtor will guide you through inspections, tests, and repair negotiations. The appraisal is important to the lender and to you, but you have plans or a vision that will make it more valuable to you, especially if you are remodeling. Look for the potential.

In addition to the CMA from your realtor, you will need to perform your own market analysis as we discussed before for the business you will be running. The building is only real estate. Housing tenants is your business that generates income. What is the potential income it will produce? Are the rents in line with what the current market will bear? If they are not as much as you hoped, hopefully you can still qualify, and sometimes they can be reported as what they should be, and what you will charge instead of what they are currently. An empty apartment is still considered for its potential. Can you see potential for increasing the income? How long has it been since the rents were analyzed? Rents increase with inflation. Sometimes with long-term tenants, rents may remain constant for many years. You will look for ways to increase income.

Rentals can give you security and bring you through a *down* economy. True, you must stay on top of things. A fourplex is usually the best option. It is the highest number of units allowed for residential loan programs, such as VA, FHA, or a conventional loan. (More than four units will put you into the commercial category and that usually means a much higher down payment and higher interest rates.)

Basically, you want to consider if the property is currently bringing in enough to pay the new payment and utilities *and* have a cushion for repairs and general maintenance. Will the property carry its own weight, or will you have to supplement it? Supplementing it is not necessarily a bad thing. We need to look at the whole picture. You need to determine what kind of a property will work for you. If you are just starting out, an affordable fourplex will be much like living in an apartment. A duplex or triplex may be more comfortable if you have a family or need a larger space. You may give up some of the income but still supplement your mortgage payment, a small price for comfort. Rentals are usually considered supplemental income and your real wealth is in the leverage you gain during the life of the investment.

Price and value are not necessarily the same thing. What is your business plan? This is not information the lender will ask for; however, compiled properly it is a useful tool for you and will be crucial if owner financing is an option. It will be part of the package we will put together in preparation for your purchase. The property you choose will be determined mostly by the preapproved price determined by your lender. As I said before that is roughly three times your annual income, plus 90% of the proposed rental income times three. Getting rid of car payments and petty bills will increase this amount. The price may be important to your lender, realtor, and appraiser but what you are concerned about is the value, the income, and the payments. The payments are what you must qualify for. You may need to consider if rents have kept up with the market's demand.

Your realtor can advise you if you should offer an amount lesser than the asking price. She will consider things like days on market (DOM), how many such properties exist in similar condition, and how hot is the market. Your realtor can give you a fairly good idea of what is going on. Trust your realtor, but do not be afraid to ask questions. If everything is selling in 90 days or less, that means some are selling in one or two days. Make a serious bid quickly on properties you are serious about. Plan your strategy with your realtor.

Depending on the volatility of the market and/or the scarcity of the properties you like, it may be wise to offer the price they ask. Many people think they should automatically offer less. This is not fair, in fact it is kind of silly. If the property is priced correctly and the CMA verifies it, you should go ahead and pay it. The few thousand dollars you save will probably not matter much over a period of thirty years. So, unless your debt ratio is too tight, offer the asked price. In a hot market, properties can move quickly. Like I said if it meets your dreams everyone else wants it too. This happens and once it has gone it is gone. Even if you do win over a few thousand dollars. The angst you cause could be more damaging since the negotiations have only begun. The experience of the realtor is crucial here.

Many times, people have found a home that meets all their criteria, and they offer less than the asking price even when advised not to. The counters may go back and forth until they are turned down or they may just get turned down from the start. Inevitably they settle for a lesser house and pay more for it. Shopping for real estate is exhausting. Do not waste everybody's time including your own. Let your realtor educate you about current prices and do your own research. Research the market, it changes fast and frequently. Although your realtor has the MLS, you have other resources such as private listing companies, i.e., *Zillow.com*, the local newspaper and internet companies such as *Craigslist*. These are plentiful, and can provide valuable information.

Offers and counteroffers can go back and forth. But once you have agreed on a price and settlement date, you want to provide the signed contract to your lender. Your realtor will send them the contract, and at that point the loan officer will probably lock your rate. The clock is ticking. Both the contract and the rate lock have expiration dates that you do not want to expire.

INSPECTIONS AND TESTS VS. APPRAISALS

We will not go into contracts too much, that is the realtors' jobs, but the inspection is something worth mentioning. You will have about a week, or whatever your contract specifies, to have it inspected by a professional inspector, a contractor or yourself if you feel qualified. You *definitely* want to be present. Follow the inspector around and ask about everything. It is better to see and understand when you are there onsite. Reading it with the photos is a good reminder. And it is vital that you to read it from one end to the other. This inspection is independent of the lender and the appraisal inspection. The home inspector you will hire is specifically looking for damage and will inspect in depth. If you do not know of one, ask your realtor to refer one. Not all inspectors are created equal so it may be a good idea to interview one. You want to know about the foundation and other structural components, as well as electrical and plumbing. This inspection is at your expense, and it is good to know if the inspector is up on current building codes and knows when each code was put into effect. You do not want a list of possible violations that may or may not be against current codes. In an older building, the codes may have changed since it was built, but are not necessarily required to be changed. The inspector needs to be well versed in this. You need to know what needs to be updated and what can be left alone. Unfortunately, some states have little or no requirements to certify the inspector's background or practices, and some inspectors will note items that they are not sure about as a way to protect themselves. This does not help you and causes a lot of confusion and wastes a lot of time.

Usually, properties are priced in accordance with age and condition; however, all health and safety items must be corrected before the loan closes. If the seller refuses, you will probably have to walk away with an FHA or VA loan, but they will probably have to fix it to qualify for any other financing. Health and safety repairs requirements are standard. At this point you can walk away and still get your earnest money back. Note: If a property is in a condition too poor to qualify for a VA or FHA loan, a short-term owner finance could be an option. You may need a resume, references, or a photo of work you have done previously. After repairs or remodel is completed, you can refinance it with a lender. You will still need the same file we are building.

When the inspections are complete and all repairs and conditions have been met, your lender will order an appraisal, and your realtor has ordered the other inspections: septic, well, furnace, etc. The appraisal and inspections are usually required to be paid upfront. In Alaska, the seller generally pays for the appraisal.

Rates

What is all this hype about rates? One of the first things I had to learn as a new loan officer was how rates work. Rates are not so complicated, but it seems few people truly understand them. I will not go into a long, complicated story here, we will just touch on the parts that directly affect your loan, but know that the first thing your loan officer does every morning is check the rates. If changes come through later in the day, they get the notification right away.

Rates can change every day and sometimes change a few times a day. Sometimes people watch them closely refusing to lock until they drop. The problem is that if they go up, you find out about it after they go up and it is too late. Not only did you not get the good rate you were hoping for, your lock must now be an even higher rate!

When you find the right property, make the purchase, even if you miss the lowest rate, don't qualify for it, or you found the perfect property when the rates are up. Not uncommon since low rates seem to drive prices up and high rates seem to level them off. And that is what will happen. You will start off with the higher rate, but as rates come down, prices again rise, and you have now gained equity. As other prices go up, your value rises too. Now, providing you have kept your credit stellar and your debt ratio intact, you can refinance at a lower rate, have a lower LTV (loan-to-value) which may remove mortgage insurance, and you get the best of both economies.

A bank may have a vault full of money, but mortgage brokerages do not. I would have thought everyone knew that, but when I was manager of The Mortgage Store in Washington State, we were actually broken into! They climbed in the very high back window, then not finding any cash, they took someone's personal laptop.

In fact, the lender does not deal with cash at all. Everything is online and on paper. Your lender facilitates the transaction, and it was explained to me this way: When you apply to borrow money and you lock your interest rate, your lender basically orders the money you need from the Feds. The Feds *earmark* the funds for you at the interest rate it was locked at. When your loan closes and the title is recorded in your name, the funds are released to your seller. If the rates rise, you still get the rate you locked in at. Unfortunately, if the rates fall, you still get the rate you are locked at. If your lock is close to expiring, there usually is a cost added to extend it even if rates have dropped. This will cost you in points or raise your rate. Your interest rate is locked by the loan officer—usually when the underwriter approves your application—but not necessarily. When your rate is locked, you qualified at that rate. If your lock expires and you have to accept a higher rate, it could ruin your debt ratio (DTI) and disqualify you.

Now Your Loan Meets the Underwriter... (But Not You)

The loan officer is under legal constraints to submit your loan package to processing whether it is complete or not—usually within 24 hours; however, if it requires additional documents, it will be logged in and returned to her where it may sit in a long row of loans undergoing the same requirements—until you produce the needed documents. Sorry, this is a big business with a lot of participants. Irritating an underwriter with an incomplete loan application package is not a good idea. Everybody loves a well-prepared borrower.

One of the most common misconceptions is that people seem to think the loan is being cultivated or is processing while it sits. If you have already been guilty of this, do not feel bad, you and 90% of borrowers have also done it. I did it once myself before I was a loan officer. The phone call went something like this:

> Me: Hello. How is my loan coming?
> Loan Officer: Let me check. I am waiting for those two documents I requested.
> Me: Yes, I know but how is it coming?

Trust me, nothing is happening, and nothing will happen until your loan application package is complete, but the clock is ticking! The underwriter will not even see your file until it is complete. The processor assembles the loan for the loan officer and sets up the file, which is quite complicated and consists of confidential information about you as well as an accumulation of documents about your chosen property.

The underwriter may approve or deny hundreds of loans every month. Time is in short supply, and they are under pressure. She does not sit with her finger holding your file open while she waits for the requested documents. In fact, if the loan is submitted and she finds an unanswered question that could disqualify you, she will stop right there and return the loan to the loan officer. This means your loan is *denied*, although if your rate has not expired, the processor and loan officer may still have time to scramble and restructure the loan or require that you provide backup documents to resolve the conflict—but realize *time is of the essence!* Time is very costly when the clock is ticking. It can cost dearly if you must extend your rate lock or lose your good rate. Rates change daily—and sometimes several times a day if the market is volatile—and sometimes they can change dramatically. The points or costs behind the rates also change. Do not take a chance! Once they change, it is too late. In fact, once you get the information, it is too late. Trust your loan officer but again, do not be afraid to ask questions.

When the loan file gets to the underwriter it should be complete. The underwriter does not know you and probably will not ever see you. Underwriters are not paid on commission. Everything is black-and-white facts. She is to remain unbiased and judge the loan on its own merits. Although we may think of her as the devil's advocate as though she is looking for any reason why she must turn you down, in reality she is. She is bound to uphold the standards of the industry and follow the guidelines set forth by the lending institution, and if your file does not comply with those guidelines, you do not qualify, and she will promptly return it to the loan officer as a DFT (Deal Fell Through). Why would she continue with a loan that does not qualify for approval when so many others are waiting for an answer also? Your loan can be denied because of lack of documentation. The loan officer or processor can further document or explain if they still have time. That is why you want to keep the additional documents handy such as bankruptcy or divorce settlements, as well as *letters of explanation* outlined below. Even though they have not and may not be requested.

The processor and loan officer will set your loan application up according to the published guidelines anticipating what the underwriter will need to see. The basic requirements, rules and regulations are published. They know these already—but each loan application can be as different as the person applying. There will be additional documents and/or tests that you, your realtor, or the seller's realtor need to provide quickly and if you do not respond quickly your rate will expire and your loan could be denied.

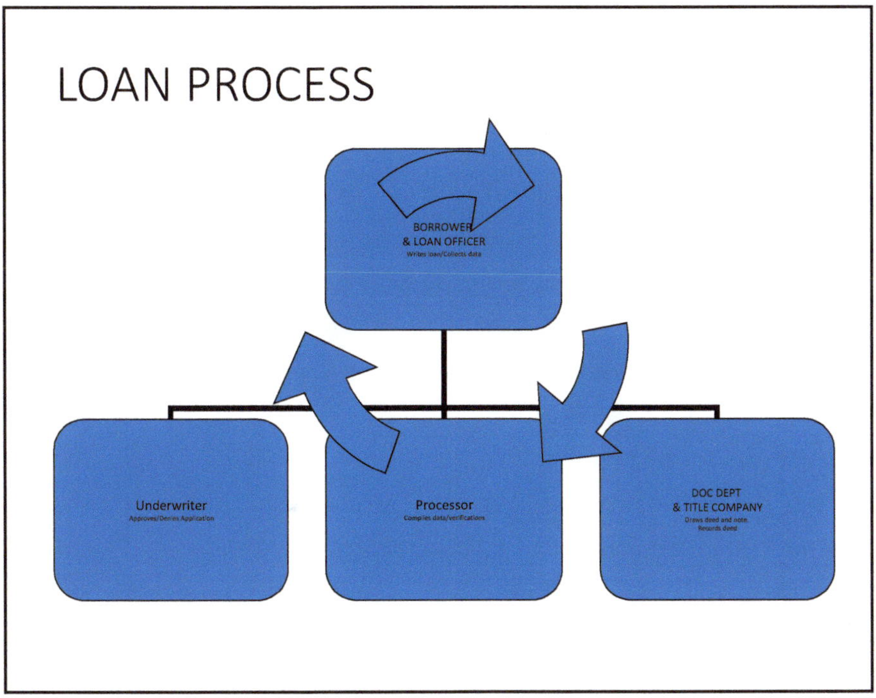

Example of how an incomplete file goes through Underwriting

Income Requirements

Besides your basic household income, and depending on your loan program, your lender will allow you to count 75% of the projected rental income as your income and sometimes up to 90%. You will add this to your current income to qualify for a loan.

In the example below the lender would most likely allow you to combine up to 90% of the $3000 rental revenue received with your total income, thereby, increasing your purchasing power by $97,200.

(($3000 x 90% = $2700)12 months = $32,400) 3 = $97,200. (Gross income X 3 is tentatively the loan amount you will qualify for....)

Therefore, if the fourplex costs $300,000 and your total gross annual family income is $67,600, you would qualify by multiplying that income times three ($202,800) plus $97,200, which equals $300,000. These numbers are subject to change, depending on underwriting guidelines and are used here as rough qualifications. The mortgage payment on $300k is dependent on the interest rate. The example below is an actual purchase that happened years ago, and the numbers were as shown below. Even if you double or triple these numbers, the percentages will be similar.

An example of an ideal fourplex purchase would have an income of $4000 and a payment of $2000. Since you will live in one of the units, you will only receive $3000 income, but you will have no outgoing mortgage payment other than the payment for the property—so it is kind of like receiving $4000. Your rents received would pay the mortgage and the utilities. True, your utilities would cost probably only $300 in this example, but let the overage accumulate. Soon enough you will have to pay for maintenance, an emergency repair, or a vacancy. Upkeep is paramount! Your job is to protect your investment and your goal is to survive the current economy whether it is good or bad. Keep it rented and charge deposits even if you must split it between months. Eventually a down economy will get better.

The good news here is that FHA and VA loans programs usually allow you to include up to 90% of your proposed rents as your own income!

The following list notes some characteristics of government-backed loans:

- 3.5% down payment for FHA and zero for VA loans
- 75 to 90% of rental income qualifies as your income.
- One-year owner-occupancy requirement
- Only one FHA and/or VA loan at a time
- You do NOT have to be first-time homebuyer!
- Homebuyers qualify for first-time homebuyers' programs if they have not owned a home in three years.
- One year of steady employment (or proof of education or training certificate)
- One year of clean credit (can build credit or provide LOXs)
- Taxes, hazard insurance and MIP are included in mortgage payment.

The flowchart below shows the general flow of the lending process at the ground level, the part that you interact with and then comes the underwriter....

The underwriter is the one who makes the final determination as to whether you qualify or not, and frequently receives the proverbial dirty look, but underwriters have strict guidelines that they are required to adhere to. Underwriters do not technically "approve" or "disapprove" your loan, you either qualify or you do not. If you qualify, you are approved. Underwriters are not your friend, or your enemy and you will almost certainly never meet them, and for good reasons. The underwriter sees only black-and-white paperwork. They do not know you and their decisions are based solely on data. They have been hired by the lender to determine with no bias if borrowers qualify or not. But underwriters are people too and many issues come down to a judgment call. A well-written explanation with proper documentation can sway a borderline decision.

That is why it is so important to write letters and explain any bad credit, job gaps, hardships, etc. A good time to do it is while you are waiting for your credit to be established or repaired. These may take a few days. Take the time to write a good competent letter or letters and keep them in a file ready for use. Stick to facts—but do not skimp on the details that will help you. Your loan officer will identify what is pertinent to the underwriter, and what you should leave out. Frequently in hardship cases, emotions and frustrations can be the proverbial *straw that breaks the camel's back*. People who are critically injured or sick may actually have funds but are too sick to manage them. Underwriters are people too and they can understand this. Your main concern is to convince them that you are responsible and have taken steps to protect yourself so that if the situation arises again, you will be protected and will not lose the property you are purchasing.

An ideal flowchart for the loan department is below. A quick overview of a typical mortgage company is as follows: You the borrower go to the loan officer, or originator, who helps you apply for a loan. To qualify for a loan, you must apply and prove specific requirements, which your loan officer will guide you through. If you are prepared when you make your appointment, your flowchart should resemble the one below. Borrower and originator complete the application and collect data to verify accuracy and obtain your DTI ratio, which consists of several steps:

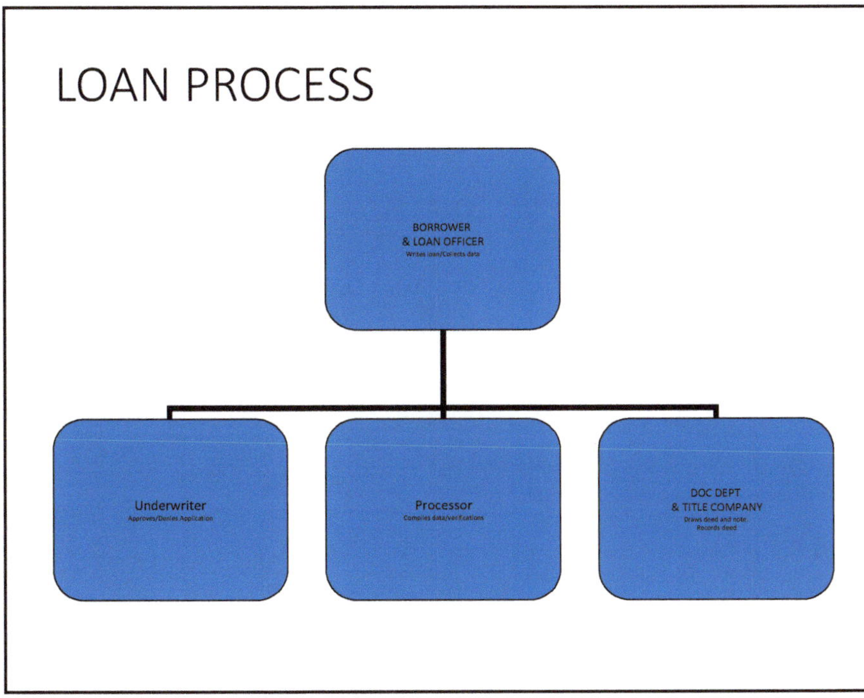

Example of a well-structured loan file.

After Closing on the Perfect Property

By the time you've closed, you've considered if the property is currently bringing in enough to pay the new payment and utilities *and* have a cushion for repairs and general maintenance. You know if the property carries its own weight, or if you have to supplement it.

After this first round ruling, can you ensure it will work? Most tenants who default on rent or demolish your property do so because of bad habits—not bad intentions. This can be costly. Protect yourself at all costs. Choose your tenants carefully and always charge a deposit. Sometimes references are available and believable and other times you will appreciate the security of charging the first and last month's rent plus a security deposit, or whatever your state laws allow. In Alaska, we currently can charge the security deposit up to the amount of the monthly rent, plus additional unspecified amounts for pets. You cannot charge additional for children. There is no proviso on how much you can charge for pets.

Consider pets carefully. Depending on your property, you may find it best to not allow any pets. Not all pet owners are responsible. Some of them have no idea that the cute little fluffy puppy would turn into a big hairy monster that smells bad, has bad manners, bothers the neighbors, leaks on your carpet, and scratches up the doors. Have the owners had them for a while and what do they do with them when they are at work? Have they been neutered? Will the pets be cared for in a way that the neighbors would not be disturbed? Pets can wreak havoc with your other tenants and with your property. Your contract will warn that the deposit does not limit payment of the damages caused by the pet; however, it is much easier to charge it upfront or turn down the applicant. After they move out, it would take a court action to be reimbursed for your repairs and that only works if they have enough money and care about their credit scores. Avoid this! Get references and charge a deposit or do not allow the pet. On the other hand, you do not want to lose a great tenant who is very responsible and has owned the pet for years. References and deposits are your best protection.

Here again, you may need to also consider if rents have kept up with the market's demand.

Now is the time to introduce yourself to your new tenants in writing and deliver in person if possible. The letter should include instructions on how and where to pay rent. You may also want to have them sign new applications and contracts, but their current contracts must be honored, until changed with proper notice. Tenants can get very nervous when their home changes owners. If you are raising the rent, you must give at least 30 days' notice, but 60 is so much better. Better yet only raise the rent with new tenants. Now is a good time to establish your own rules. Protect your property by keeping your grounds clean! State it in the *enforceable* contract. Do not allow clutter—not only does it degrade your property--tenants don't always take it with them! Car repairs must be completed in short, specified time periods and remain in running condition. Non-running cars must be removed. People keep tires when they change to studs but frequently leave them behind. If you allow tires with special permission, they must be stored out of sight, and identified with tenants' name. Tires and other large items are hard to identify to charge tenant—but you will have to remove them at your expense. Enforce your contract by using forms from *The Landlord-Tenant Act* for legal actions.

There is no standard application or contract. The first one I used, came with the tenants of the first property I bought. It was several pages of legal sounding jargon, which seemingly the tenants found tiresome and disregarded. Finally, as I rotated through tenants, I cut it down to a couple of pages. You don't have to restate the law. You are dealing with adults and they are expected to know right from wrong. Most things are covered in the *Landlord-Tenant Act*, which supersedes your contract. The basic laws always supersede any contract. You need the tenants' contact information, contract dates and other information pertinent to the individual contract. For example, you may want to limit the number and condition of cars each apartment is allowed or include a reminder about posted Quiet Hours. Too much jargon and the content will be lost. Keep it simple. Excessive noise and illegal activity are already illegal and are covered in the Landlord-Tenant Act.

Maintenance, Maintenance, Maintenance

- Establish routine maintenance
    - Changes filters, check appliances, etc
    - Keep premises orderly and in good repair
- State it in the contract. Contracts are enforceable!
    - Refer to Landlord-Tenant Act for legal forms/actions
    - Provide garbage service
    - Do not allow clutter—they don't take it with them!
        - Car repairs must be completed in short specified period and remain in running condition.
        - Tires may be allowed with special permission, stored out of wight, and identified with tenants' name. They are hard to identify and charge tenant and no one ever claims them!

SAMPLE

NOTICE TO TENANT OF INCREASE IN RENT OF MONTH-TO-MONTH TENANCY

To: ______________________________ ______________________________
(Tenant) (Date)

Re: ______________________________
(Address of rental unit)

____
(City, State)

You are notified that your rent will increase to $__________ per month effective on the rental due date at least 30 days from the date you receive this notice. Your rent is due on the ________ day of each month, so this increase will take effect on ______________________, 20____.

You may elect to either accept this increase or move. If you choose to move, you must provide me a written notice of termination of the tenancy at least 30 days prior to the rental due date when you plan to move.

Signed: ______________________________
(Landlord/Property Manager)

Landlord's Record of Service

Instructions: Serve a copy of this notice on the tenant. Immediately fill out this section to describe how service was accomplished. Complete all statements that apply. Keep the completed original.

□ Tenant acknowledges receipt of this notice on _______. ______________________
(Date) (Tenant's Signature)

□ This notice was personally served on ________________ by the undersigned on _______.
(Name) (Date)

□ I attempted to make personal service on the tenant. I knocked on the door, but no one answered. I believed the landlord was absent, so I securely affixed the notice to the entry door of the premises. This was done on the _____ day of __________, 20___ at __________ o'clock a.m./p.m.

□ Tenant was served by registered or certified mail. (I have retained the receipt.)

Date:_________ Signature:________________________ Print Name: ______________

Keep a copy of this notice.

39

SAMPLE

NOTICE TO TENANT OF TERMINATION OF TENANCY FOR VIOLATION OF AGREEMENT/LAW

To: ______________________________ (Tenant) ______________________________ (Date)

Re: ______________________________ (Address of rental unit)

______________________________ (City, State)

You are notified that you have seriously violated your rental agreement with me or your duties under the law. The violation(s) is/are specifically as follows:

____

____

____

□ If you do not remedy the violation(s) listed above by: ______________________________

____

____

____

(explanation of remedial action to be taken by tenant to correct violation)

within TEN DAYS of the date you receive this notice, your tenancy will terminate, and you must move. Failure to remedy the violations listed here will mean that you must move out by the ______ day of __________, 20____, at ________ o'clock a.m./p.m. If you have not remedied the problem(s) and have not moved out by the date above, a lawsuit may be filed to evict you. If you remedy the problem(s) within ten days, you may stay. If the same problem occurs again within 6 months, you may be given a notice to terminate the tenancy and you will not be given an opportunity to fix the problem.

□ Since this is substantially the same violation for which you were previously given notice within the past six months on the __ day of ___, I am electing to terminate your tenancy on _____, which is at least FIVE DAYS from the date you receive this notice.

Signed: ______________________________ (Landlord/Property Manager)

Landlord's Record of Service

Instructions: Serve a copy of this notice on the tenant. Immediately fill out this section to describe how service was accomplished. Complete all statements that apply. Keep the completed original.

□ Tenant acknowledges receipt of this notice on _______ (Date). ____________________ (Tenant's Signature)

□ This notice was personally served on __________________ (Name) by the undersigned on _______ (Date).

□ I attempted to make personal service on the tenant. I knocked on the door, but no one answered. I believed the landlord was absent, so I securely affixed the notice to the entry door of the premises. This was done on the _____ day of __________, 20___ at __________ o'clock a.m./p.m.

□ Tenant was served by registered or certified mail. (I have retained the receipt.)

Date:_________ Signature:_________________________ Print Name: _______________

Keep a copy of this notice.

Taxes

A person should pay exactly what he owes. Not a penny more and not a penny less. Not sure where I heard that, but it sounds like a good idea when it comes to taxes. Take advantage of the tax laws; they will help you.

Tax laws can be your best friend and your worst enemy. The IRS laws allow depreciation of your investment and interest, as well as repairs, supplies and expenses are deductible. These beneficial laws are very inspiring to small family entrepreneurs' wanting to supplement income.

Always open a separate bank account and keep it separate from other accounts. Security deposits should be kept in a separate non-interest-bearing account.

Accountants charge by the hour so initial instructions may save you a lot of money. Make an appointment and meet with a tax professional for an overview of the specific tax benefits and requirements of your investments. It is not necessary to memorize—all these benefits are yours whether you know about them or not, and the overview itself can be found online. But this is a big subject, and your primary concentration should be on running the business. Let someone else do your taxes. Your accountant may be helpful in setting up your accounting practices. A good accounting or record-keeping system can save you a great deal of time, money, and confusion.

You want to find an accountant you can trust to carry this burden for you. That is where an interview is a good idea. Meet them when it is not tax time. In fact, about two weeks after the tax deadline and their ensuing days off is probably the best time to set up. Show up with your packet you got from the title company which will include your HUD1 statement and other documents they will need to see. Unless you are a professional CPA, lawyer, or accountant, a tax professional is a mandatory part of your new team.

According to Wikipedia:

The ***HUD-1 Settlement Statement*** *is a standard form in use in the United States of America which is used to itemize services and fees charged to the borrower by the lender or broker when applying for a loan for the purpose of purchasing or refinancing real estate. HUD refers to the Department of Housing and Urban Development.*

The borrower has the right to inspect the HUD-1 one day prior to day of settlement. The form is filled out by the settlement agent who will conduct the settlement.

Since 2010, the HUD-1 settlement statement also contains what is referred to as a Good Faith Estimate or GFE. This additional set of figures specifies estimated settlement figures provided by the lender upon application of the loan.

Borrowers may compare their Good Faith Estimate to the HUD-1 Settlement Statement and ask their lender or broker about any changes.

As part of new rules established by the CFPB effective October 3, 2015, the HUD-1 Settlement Statement became obsolete. It has been replaced by a document called the Closing Disclosure that consolidates the HUD-1, Good Faith Estimate, and Truth in Lending Act disclosures.

Look for a reputable professional who can and will take time to speak to you in terms you can understand. I would not worry too much about their charges; they are always outrageous as most professionals are, but it's money well spent and hopefully the benefits will far outweigh the expense (which is also deductible). An accountant who can advise you and of course, exercise tax laws to your advantage is an essential part of your new team.

According to the IRS official website www.IRS.gov:

Generally, each year you will report all income and deduct all out-of-pocket expenses in full. The deduction to recover the cost of your rental property—depreciation—is taken over a prescribed number of years,

Depreciation *is a capital expense. It is the mechanism for recovering your cost in an income producing property and must be taken over the expected life of the property. You can begin to depreciate rental property when it is ready and available for rent.*

Interest expense: *You can deduct mortgage interest you pay on your rental property.*

Interest can account for over 90% of your first payments—big deduction!

Now that You're an Owner – Look Out for Scammers!

Scammers come in all shapes and sizes. From the internet scammer who applies, gets you to "hold" an apartment and then sends you a check for additional funds that you are requested to deposit and refund the excess to them. Checks sent can have the appearance of a real check—but never make a refund. The tenant must stop payment and issue another check for the correct amount. A scammer will disappear at this point.

The other scammers you need to watch for are those tenants who feel they have entitlements. You want to stick closely to the state Landlord-Tenant Law. When in doubt over a dispute or question, always take the moral highroad. But watch for people who try to scam, disrupt, or complain nonstop about petty annoyances. One negative tenant can cause good tenants to move because of the constant negativity. Or even instigate trouble between them. When you buy an established multifamily home, it may very well be occupied. Although you want to be fair, there is to my knowledge no rule that every contract must match. You may waive an annual rent increase for a long-term tenant *because* of their tenancy, where a new tenant may pay the updated rent.

One such purchase I made was occupied in three units, each with a different contract with different rates and in different stages of their tenancy. As the new owner, I introduced myself in a hand-delivered letter and gave them all new instructions as to where rent and communications should be directed but did not change any contracts immediately. Any changes would require 30 days' notice and were eventually all updated, but in the meantime, some of them were paying utilities and some were not.

The previous owner had originally required that tenants pay their own utilities, and the apartments were on separate meters so they could. Why did the one tenant not pay them? Possibly in a crunch to fill a vacancy, the owner had included utilities in rent. If the market slows down for a few months, you cannot afford to wait on the next surge to fill an empty apartment. Your mortgage payments are due as usual. Probably the utilities arrangement was the dealmaker. At any rate, when I filled the one vacancy, the tenant signed the contract with the updated rate and was responsible for her own utilities. She was seemingly happy as she signed into the utility companies. But tenants talk and about three weeks later, while at work, I received a phone call from the new tenant. "Why are some of us paying utilities and others aren't?" she demanded. Then before I could answer, she quickly added, "Don't lie! We're all here and listening to you." Apparently, she had assembled some of the other tenants and the worst part was that she had not paid rent at all! She had paid her security deposit and I had agreed to trade her first month's rent for her painting the apartment. The apartment required paint and I was too busy with my job to do it myself and because she said she had worked in the industry and was related to and recommended by another tenant who often did handywork for me, it seemed like a good choice.

There were only two of them present during the phone call, but a couple of days later the upstairs tenant who had been there for a few years called and asked why she was the *only* one paying utilities. At this point, I felt I had to act. All the contracts were updated with proper forms and the proper notice. The troublemaker had not paid her rent or painted the apartment, so I gave her the 7-day notice. When she did not pay, I filed for a court date. It was my first eviction and apparently, she had intended to meet me in court with everyone's contracts. Not that it would have mattered because I was knowledgeable about the law and was on the right side of it. She was from California and that may be a valid reason there for not paying rent there, but in Alaska it is not. And there is no law that says you must charge rent or raise rents equally if it is not discrimination. You can trade rent for work and/or you could let friends live for free if you want. Frequently landlords do not raise rents for faithful long-term tenants that take care of your property. New tenants get the new rate. Had she showed up it would have done her no good.

As it turned out she did not even show. Our court date was set for a Tuesday morning. Unfortunately, Monday had been a holiday and she had mistakenly thought Tuesday was Monday and was prepared to show up the next day. She shared this with me when I brought her the judge's order to be out in 24 hours. She was out within 24 hours.

Quarrelsome tenants are sometimes the hardest to remove. You really do not want to lose tenants for any reason and general rules should be posted or included in the contract—even those that go without saying—like being quiet at night. But if you are inundated with constant petty complaints about other tenants, a possible solution is to introduce tenants to each other and exit the scene. If it continues invite them to turn in notice and move, and if that does not cure it, give them a 30-day notice. If they have paid their rent timely and taken care of the place, they will get their security deposit back. You are not their mother. How much of your valuable time do you want to waste?

One tenant invited me in to show me that her three preschool-age children had used color crayons on the wall, and to compensate, she had demanded that they use a pail of water and wash it off. I think she wanted me to approve of her parenting style. I did not and was horrified that not only was my wall damaged, but now water was also being soaked into my carpet. I gulped and left the apartment. What else could I do?

A tenant once texted a photo of the waste she had removed from the vacuum cleaner I left stored in the unit! I do not know what she intended but at 4:30 in the morning it turned my stomach. I took the opportunity to clarify her that the vacuum had actually been left for my convenience and she was welcomed to use it or not, but it was not part of the rental agreement, and if she was going to use it, she should clean it!

The first couple of months she complained nonstop that the other tenants were annoying her, weeds were growing in front of her home, and she demanded that someone clean them up—after all, she paid rent! She even gave some orders to the maintenance person, which he found quite irritating, and before long they were at each other's throats. She complained nonstop, and he did everything he could to irritate her. I gave him a couple of notices but finally told them to get over it or move out. Sometimes a firm invitation to "put in 30-days' notice" and move is the best way to handle an instigator. I pointed out that her surroundings, weeds, and all were her responsibility to keep up, per her contract. Surprisingly after a few complaints, she turned out to be a good tenant, always paying her rent on time, taking took good care of my place and she made friends with the maintenance man's wife. Some people think of you as their surrogate mother, and will complain to you even before, or rather than meet their neighbors.

West Coast Laws are Similar But Can Vary

The Alaska Landlord-Tenant Act is simply stated, and the first paragraph outlines the intent clearly. This is a wonderful philosophy, and it is exactly how you want to run your business.

When a landlord and tenant get along well, things are better all around. Dealing with unhappy tenants is a lot of trouble for a landlord, and few tenants want the inconvenience and expense of moving simply because they cannot get along with their landlords. Yet, landlords and tenants frequently have problems. Sometimes, landlords do not make repairs or unfairly keep back security deposits. Sometimes, tenants damage property or refuse to pay the rent. This publication briefly explains your responsibilities as a landlord or a tenant under the Uniform Residential Landlord and Tenant Act (AS 34.03.010 et seq., the "Landlord and Tenant Act").

The following excerpts are points of interest for this publication; however, you will want to read it through completely and refer to it often. Forms for legal actions for both tenants and landlords are provided in the back of the book and can be photocopied or reprinted to look more professional, but they should include the same language.

Many landlords demand a security deposit before a tenant moves in. This deposit protects the landlord from financial loss if the tenant fails to pay the rent, causes damage to the property, or does not clean up properly when he or she leaves. Except for units renting for more than $2,000 per month, security deposits and prepaid rents may not total more than two months' rent.

Deposits and prepaid rent must be deposited by the landlord or the property manager in a trust account in a bank or savings and loan association, or with a licensed escrow agent. (Exceptions could be made in rural Alaska, if there is no bank in town and it would be impractical to bank the money.) A trust account can be any separate savings or checking account labeled "trust account" and used only for deposits and prepaid rents. A receipt should be written whenever the tenant pays a deposit or prepays rent. Landlords are required to provide tenants with the terms and conditions under which prepaid rents or deposits (or any portion of those monies) might be withheld by the landlord.

A seven-day written notice is required to terminate a tenancy when a tenant is behind in rent. The notice must state the correct amount of rent to be paid by the tenant. If the rent is paid before the seven complete days are up, then the tenant may stay. (If the tenant tries to pay after the seven days are up, the landlord may refuse to accept the rent and continue with the eviction.) The notice must tell tenants that they have the choice of paying or moving. If a landlord accepts a partial rent payment after giving a seven-day notice for nonpayment, the landlord must either make a new written agreement with the tenant to extend the eviction for a specific period of time or begin the eviction process all over again.

A minimum 24-hour written notice must be given to terminate a tenancy when the tenant or the tenant's guests have intentionally caused more than $400 damage to the landlord's property. Even if the tenant agrees to repair the damage (and the tenant will be liable for the damage in any event), the landlord may still go through with the eviction.

If the tenant agrees to pay for the damage, why would you want to evict them? Are there extenuating circumstances? I guess it is a good *out* if you have other concerns. Especially if it was due to fighting. Fighting is undoubtedly the worst thing that can happen to your property. And if they have had more than one offense, evict them.

A ten-day written notice is required when the landlord wishes to terminate a tenancy because the tenant has breached an important part of the rental agreement or the tenant's responsibilities under the Landlord and Tenant Act (such as disturbing other tenants with too much noise or failing to maintain the rental unit, so that the health and safety of others are endangered). If the problem is corrected before expiration of the notice period, the tenant may stay. However, if the tenant violates the rental agreement in substantially the same way more than once in a six-month period, the landlord can evict the tenant with a five-day notice, and the tenant has no right to fix the problem.

According to the law, rental agreements must require that tenants notify their landlord every time they plan to be gone for more than seven days. If the tenant plans to be gone only two or three days, then finds he will actually be gone for more than a week, the tenant must notify the landlord as soon as possible. This is to help protect the property from damage such as that caused by freezing pipes. Tenants who willfully fail to give notice of being gone can be sued by their landlord for 1½ times the actual damages caused by any calamity occurring during their absence.

The Oregon law reads as follows (excerpts only):

The most common deposit a landlord may require is a security deposit. Security deposits protect the landlord if the tenant fails to pay the rent or causes damage to the rental premises beyond ordinary wear and tear. Your landlord cannot charge you for normal wear and tear. In Oregon, there is no minimum or maximum amount your landlord can charge for the security deposit. A landlord is required to provide a tenant with a receipt for the security deposit. Your landlord does not have to pay you the interest earned on your security deposit.

Your security deposit must be personally delivered or mailed within 31 days. If your landlord wrongfully keeps part or all of the money, you have up to one year to settle the matter or file a lawsuit for up to twice the amount of the money your landlord kept.

When rent is more than 7 days overdue, you may give the tenant a written notice stating your intent to try to evict him or her if the rent is not paid within 72 hours. You can give a similar notice, for

144 hours, on the 5th day the rent is overdue if you prefer. If a tenant (or someone in the tenant's control) harms you or your property, harms other people on the property, or commits an act that is outrageous in the extreme, you may give the tenant a 24-hour notice to leave. The notice must be in writing in a special legal form. It needs to explain the reason for termination, and it must be delivered personally to the tenant or mailed to the tenant by first-class mail only. If a notice is mailed, you must add three days to the notice time. The legal form of the notice must be correct in all details in order to be enforced in court.

If the tenant ignores most of your notices and you want the tenant to move out, you must file an eviction complaint in court. The tenant will be properly served with a summons and complaint. There will be a hearing and possibly a trial where you can ask that the tenant be evicted. If the judge or jury agrees, you will be granted a judgment entitling you to possession of the property. If the tenant still does not move, you must pay the sheriff to come to the property to remove the tenant, and you must be responsible for temporarily storing any of the tenant's remaining property until you make reasonable efforts to give the belongings back and they become legally "abandoned." Rights regarding such situations are complicated, and getting legal advice is a good idea. Read "When Tenants Leave Belongings Behind" in this series for more information.

When I looked up the California law this is the first notice that popped up. The only comment I have here is that you should always keep your premises clean and in good repair. Something is really wrong if you are in danger of any of these actions!

***Tenants** may withhold rent, move out without notice, sue the **landlord**, call state or local health inspectors, or exercise the right to "repair and deduct" if a **landlord** fails to take care of important repairs, such as a broken heater. For specifics: see **California Tenant Rights** to Withhold Rent or "Repair and Deduct."*

The *repair and deduct* right referred to here means simply that if you do not make required health or safety repairs timely, your tenant can pay for the repairs needed (such as furnace repair) and deduct them dollar for dollar from rent. This may be a good option for a novice landlord, but don't force it on them. They pay the same either way but request the agreement when they first report it and only as a last resort! They also have the option to break a lease and move out. That would mean no rent, no new renter and still the furnace must be repaired before you can collect rent!

This would underscore the importance of routine inspections and maintenance. Furnaces and other such utility malfunctions usually happen the first week of winter, understandably, as soon as the temperature drops! All repair people are on overtime and may have to schedule you for next week! This lends to higher *emergency* repair costs, or temporary fixes until you can pay for a permanent one and that could cost you twice as much. Stay on top of things! You can lose a lot here.

The California law does not specify how late the rent must be but states the following:

In the case of nonpayment of rent, the tenant must be given a three-day notice demanding that the rent in default be paid or, in the alternative, that the property be surrendered to the landlord. The exact amount of rent in default must be specified. In the case of a breach of another lease covenant, the tenant must be given a three-day notice demanding that the lease covenant be performed, and the breach be stopped, if that is possible. For example, in the case of a no-pet clause, the tenant must be given three days to remove the pet {Code of Civil Procedure Sec. 1161}.

The California law covers a multitude and is extremely specific about other rights.

There is no longer a formal distinction among tenant deposits, i.e., security, cleaning, last month's rent, pet, key, waterbed deposits, etc.

California recognizes only a unitary security deposit. This is defined as any advance payment to the landlord to be used to remedy defaults in rent payments, repair of damage to the premises exclusive of normal wear and tear, ... Landlords may not charge any non-refundable deposits or "fees" {Civil Code Sec. 1950.5}.

The statute implies, but does not explicitly require, that this deposit be held separate by the landlord. Payment of interest is not required by State law, but several local jurisdictions do require it. Landlords who own rentals in Berkeley, Cotati, East Palo Alto, Hayward, Los Angeles, San Francisco, Santa Cruz, Santa Monica, Watsonville and West Hollywood must pay interest to tenants on deposits. Call the applicable rent board, city clerk or apartment association for further information or requirements.

It's always a good idea to have a separate account and in California possibly a non-interest-bearing account; however, the statement does not specify that it's because of the bank paid interest you earn. If in doubt call an official or an attorney. Alaska law states you don't have to pay interest but must say so in the contract. You are required to keep security deposits in a separate account that is labeled "trust" account.

The security deposit may not exceed three months' rent if the premises are rented furnished, two months' rent if they are rented unfurnished. An amount equal to an extra one-half month's rent if the tenant has a waterbed {Civil Code Sec. 1950.5}.

I would want to have a good screening process since this allows only basic protection since the above paragraph stated that the last month's rent is considered a "deposit."

Within three weeks (21 days) of the date the tenant vacates the landlord must provide an accounting of any charges to the deposit in writing. The landlord may not charge for repairs, cleaning, etc., above and beyond reasonable wear and tear. The accounting may be mailed to the tenant's last known address together with any refund *due. Failure to do this in bad faith subjects the landlord to any actual damage suffered by the tenant, as determined by the court, plus statutory damages of up to $600 {Civil Code Sec. 1950.5}.*

Normal wear and tear usually include painting interior walls and cleaning carpets in unfurnished premises. The landlord is responsible for these.

California residential landlords are considered to be businesses within the meaning of the anti-discrimination statutes and are bound by them according to their terms.

All persons in the state are deemed to be equal and entitled to equal accommodations, advantages, etc., despite their sex, race, color, religion, ancestry, national origin or disability {Civil Code Sec. 51}. Age discrimination is specifically prohibited {Civil. Code Sec. 51.2}, although senior housing is permissible {Civil. Code Sec. 51.3}.

Many states do require business licenses. Check with your state website. As far as discrimination, I firmly believe in anti-discrimination. As a business owner, you cannot afford petty discriminations anyway. You have enough concerns. A tenant who pays timely rent, takes care of your premises, and gets along with the other tenants is priceless. Nothing else matters.

Landlords may not refuse to rent or continue to rent to tenants, with waterbeds or liquid-filled furniture, who are residing in any structure built after 1972. Landlords are protected and have the right to be present at the time of waterbed installation to inspect for the proper installation, require minimum waterbed component standards, including conformity to the floor weight load limits of the local building code and most importantly require the tenant show proof of insurance for a minimum amount of $100,00.00 {Civil. Code Sec. 1940.5}.

Wow! This brings a whole new meaning to the term California waterbed! And seriously—is a waterbed a necessity that entitles tenants to state protection? Really?

As you can see laws vary widely in the West Coast states, as I suspect does the rest of the nation. I strongly suspect laws were written because of infringements that were not specified in the law. If in doubt—consult an attorney and always play fair to the best of your ability, especially in the gray areas.

SAMPLE

LANDLORD'S SECURITY DEPOSIT OFFSET STATEMENT

To: ______________________ From: ______________________
(Tenant) (Landlord)

______________________ ______________________
(Address) (Address)

______________________ ______________________

This statement concerns the following premises:

Description: ______________________
(house, 4-plex, apartment building, trailer, trailer space, etc.)

Location: ______________________
(street address, apartment number, city and state)

This statement is made pursuant to AS 34.03.070(b). It accurately sets forth the amount of rent due and is an itemization of damages to the premises.

Date of tenant's departure from premises: ______________________
Amount of tenant deposit: $______________________

Offset for rent due landlord $ ____________
Offset for damages to premises $ ____________
Itemize the offsets below: (attach continuation sheets as necessary)

____
____
____
____

TOTAL OFFSETS (if any) $ ________
AMOUNT DUE TENANT, IF ANY (check enclosed) $ ________

______________________ Signature: ______________________
(Date) Print Name: ______________________

<u>Instructions</u>: *Provide or serve a copy of this statement to tenant at checkout or thereafter, or mail to tenant's last known address within 14 days of tenant's departure (or 30 days if costs are being deducted for damages due to tenant's noncompliance with the duties listed in AS 34.03.120). Immediately make a notation of service or mailing on the retained original and copies of this statement. Complete all that apply.*

□ *Tenant acknowledges receipt of this statement on* ______. ______________________
(Date) (Tenant's Signature)

□ *This notice was personally served on* ______________________ *by the undersigned on* ____________.
(Name of Tenant) (Date)

□ *This statement has been mailed to tenant at tenant's last known address which is set forth above. It was mailed on* ______________________.

______________________ Signature: ______________________
(Date) Print Name: ______________________

More Words to the Wise

Responsible long-term tenants will help stave off repairs, keep maintenance costs minimal and help ensure the security of your investment. You are running a business for profit. Some tenants habitually take care of their belongings and others do not—and do not even know they don't! It is up to you to protect your property! The Landlord-Tenant Act is your best reference. Always protect yourself with security deposit, references, and employment verifications. Talking to an applicant when you show the apartment will give you a feel of how responsible they are. Automobiles and how they take care of them are important clues.

Always charge a deposit and sometimes you may want to include the last month's rent. If you have approved their application but they are unable to pay rent and deposits upfront and you must split it over two months: Give a receipt for the security deposit first and then the rent. If worst comes to worst, you can evict a tenant for not paying rent, but you will still have the deposit to cover your losses. Never rent without a deposit. You are better off to give free rent then to not charge a deposit. Without a deposit, you have no recourse. The deposit can also cover the last's month if you must evict.

If you rent on a weekend and cannot reach the employer or references, ACCEPT rents, security deposit and a paycheck stub, with the understanding that if their information is false, they must move out immediately. I find people to be generally honest and have never had a problem here, but then I had a deposit to ensure it. Read the market. If it is tight you will want to accept. Always protect yourself—but do not lose the potential tenant in a tight market. Other times, prospective tenants love your property but want to look around before they plan. You can't stop them and in fact the more you protest, the less credible you will seem. Too bad when they come back, and the place has been rented. This has happened on more than one occasion. Once a woman wanted to wait for her paycheck to be delivered the next day. That seemed reasonable, but you can't always wait. I begged her to put down a small deposit, which I would not deposit until she would call the next day, but she refused. She was devastated when she returned the next day and found it had rented. I felt like crap, but holding an apartment is not always a good idea. Are they really just buying time because they are not sure? You will be left holding the bag. Generally, you have a small window at the first of the month and then everybody moves and settles down and you may have to wait another month. If a tenant qualifies and is ready to pay, accept it and sign the contract. It is not fair to either of you to wait on someone you don't even know.

Profits from rents should be reinvested in the same property. Ideally the incoming rents should equal the payment plus the averaged utilities plus a cushion of 25%. The cushion is to cover vacancies, repairs, and other unexpected expenses.

Clean and modern apartments attract people who appreciate quality and are used to keeping things neat. Habits of your tenants can make or break you. If you show a dirty apartment, they will be grossed out. I would be more worried if the applicant sees nothing wrong with the dirty apartment—unless it is the last vacant place in town.

Military tenants are typically good tenants with good secure jobs! Make sure you get the commanding officer's name and phone number. Military officials require their charges to be responsible citizens and will help you if you do have trouble.

Do you allow animals? I usually allow one small animal if applicants have references that include the pet. Pets must always be over a year old. People are happier when the have their pets and a mature pet that has been trained, is better than an undisclosed, newly acquired animal. You can charge an additional deposit for the pet and require pets be neutered or spayed, and people must have arrangements for the animal when they are at work: Do they take the pet with them? Do they leave it in a crate? And is the pet used to that kind of treatment? You do not want the neighbors to complain about animals crying or barking. Protect yourself in writing in your contract. Everybody thinks their pet is perfect. Of course, the pet does not bark when the owner is there, but when he has gone and I knock on the door, frequently the pet will ruin the interior door while it tries to scratch a hole in it! If neighbors share the same exterior entrance, this will happen every time they come home also.

Accept AHFC tenants: Usually these people were on a waiting list and have waited months! They are not likely to move soon. AHFC inspects their units on a yearly basis, and they always pay on time. The rent source is usually split between AHFC and the tenant so you will get two checks each month. The tenant knows if they are evicted for any reason they will be removed from the benefits and will not get another chance.

Should you rent to people who do not have references? Yes. Charge first, last and deposit. If they have recently sold their home, they will not have references. Ask to see the HUD1 statement. They can get a copy from their title company. Previous homeowners usually make good tenants because they have previously had to take care of a home.

Follow the Landlord-Tenant Act, a booklet written for the protection of both landlord and tenant. Become familiar with the procedures. You are running a business for profit. Protect yourself by giving proper notices, even with a verbal agreement, follow up in writing. Eviction is best to avoid completely, but if you ever must evict a tenant, do it quickly and professionally. You have a deposit equal to one month's rent so you will not lose out and you can immediately advertise and rent it again. Your tenant is free to move on. I usually do not waste time chasing lost rents. You can ruin people's credit but recovering lost rents from people who did not have the money in the first place is rather futile, even in a broken lease agreement. You will get the judgment, but *you cannot squeeze blood from a turnip.*

RENTING UNITS

- Never show a dirty apartment!
  - Advertise vacancy on Social Media, Craig's List or the local paper
  - Get a full application
  - Verify the income and references
  - Use a contract (even friends)
  - ALWAYS GET A DEPOSIT (especially friends)
  - Don't lose a good prospect: Accept rent contingent on quick verification of application.
  - Protect yourself and your property!

REFURBISH ASAP!

- Quick tricks allowed!
- Change toilet seat
- Touch up trim
- Paint center of walls with matched paint
- USE APPLIANCES
- Check all plumbing
- Wash light fixtures and globes

What Do You Do in a Pinch?

No matter how diligently you have worked, or how great your talents. One thing you cannot control is the economy. It can change at a moment's notice and so do your dreams! About four years after I had purchased my multifamily homes, things were going great. I had opened a real estate company and was plowing full steam ahead when the housing market hit a standstill! Purportedly it happened May 6, 2006. My new company with our 66 listings took a hard hit. The job market followed and some of my tenants had to move due to nonpayment of rent. I used every trick I could and was able to again rent the units, but I had slipped a month behind on the payment on my largest property and was getting close to two months. Even though I was again collecting rents I could not catch it up. It continued as a *rolling 30* for a few months. And then as if by magic, I got a call from a lender! This was a lender I had never heard of. She informed me that the government had allowed them to loan me funds at a good rate so I could catch up. She had me look up and verify her contact information. I don't remember many specifics, but my history was perfect and I qualified easily. It was independent of my mortgage, and I think it was something as simple as that I had to be at least one payment behind. To that point I had a perfect record.

I can't tell you how to even find a loan like this—but just know they are out there. The Federal government wants us to succeed, and they can help. You may want to call your lender or CPA to find out.

Desperation is the mother of invention. That whole experience started me again thinking about designing a plan for a steadier income. Perhaps a niche market? Different buildings and locations favor various occupants. Seniors prefer one level with no stairs inside or out, as do families with small children, who also prefer fenced yards. Everyone wants to be away from traffic, but employees may opt for a location close to work.

A steadier source of income is senior citizens. Senior citizens prefer single-level homes and well-kept yards, views, outdoor community areas, and covered parking. Their unit should include washer and dryer and all utilities, including cable TV and Wi-Fi. They tend to be very long-term and usually take very good care of your place. Since they are usually on a steady fixed income, timely rent is not a problem. Although they don't have children, they frequently have pets. Seniors in general seem very responsible when it comes to their pets, although it is a good idea to charge an additional deposit. Because they are the preferred tenants, rents are frequently lower for this demographic. You won't have so many turnovers or repairs. But due to the layout of my 2-story apartments, this was not a good option.

After about ten years of renting long-term apartments and breaking even, I changed to furnished, short-term rentals. I had two friends in the *cabins* business. They lived different directions, in different towns and did not know each other. One thing they both had in common is that, while I was working full-time, breaking even on rents (although living free of rent and utilities) they were also doing so, but had money to spare for upgrades and both went on lavish annual vacations they paid for themselves. They rented nightly, and although I was not set up for such high turnover, I thought I should try month-to-month and furnished. Tentatively I place my first ad for a furnished month-to-month rental with all utilities paid. This only included the actual furniture and washer/dryer. Although I raised the rent by about 35%, I rented it on the second call. I got 14 calls!

Apparently, my hunch was right: People moving are frequently going through life-changing events, such as divorce, job transfer, or they may be moving in from out of state. Relocation for any reason is a life-changing event. Usually in either of these they tend to be without home furnishings, and since they frequently are looking to buy or build, they may not want to be tied to a whole year's lease. However, it was my experience they usually stayed for most of that time.

Slightly overwhelmed by the response and the suddenness of it, I rushed to quickly furnish the apartment before I could show it. All of the furniture from my family room and extra bedroom was the first to go. It fit well into the smaller two-bedroom apartment. I finished it out with twin beds and a chest of drawers from a local used furniture store. The tenant was responsible for his own housewares. Newly separated from his marriage, he needed a quick place to move in with his son. He stayed for over a year. I had immediately converted all of my units to short-term and furnished them all, not only with furniture, but I completed them with all the housewares: linens, towels and kitchenware. I had long since learned that the washer and dryer were smart to provide because tenants always nicked and scratched the walls and doors as they moved out through the apartments' small doors and narrow stairwells, but now I provided the other culprit: the queen box springs. This new niche involved much more than matching carpets and drapes. I found some used big screen TVs to finish out the living areas. They showed very well.

Although later I did try nightly, I found it was too high of turnover for the location of my apartments. People would reserve one night, not knowing airport was over an hour away. Then when their plane landed, they would rent a car, drive for an hour to my place, do laundry and take showers, sleep for a couple of hours and head back for the airport. That wasn't the peaceful atmosphere I was geared for. The month-to-month, however, worked out so well I converted the rest of my units.

I eventually settled on short-term seasonal contracts. I found corporations frequently send summer employees which included construction companies, medical professionals, and one scientist. Basically, in the summer a superintendent flies in for the summer months. He moves in one night and reports to work the next day, where he is provided a company pickup. His rent may be reimbursed, or he may pay himself. The medical professionals are the same. They fly in, rent, or buy an auto and report to work. They work long hours and enjoy sitting and gazing at beautiful scenery while eating and watching the news. They may enjoy the gas fireplace for a while and then turn in for the night, to start again in the morning. On their few days off, they want to hike and explore the attractions of Alaska. They want a nice, clean, comfortable fully furnished home that they can move right into and then move out when their tour of duty is finished and fly off and leave everything. I found with this class, they wanted comfort and convenience as well as good TV and dependable Wi-Fi and a private outdoor deck or balcony. They would pay the price—often being reimbursed. I doubled the monthly rents and furnished the kitchens and baths completely. I included complete bedding and towels, kitchenware, and wall decor. I advertised: *All you need to bring is your toothbrush.* Most of these came from secondhand stores, yard sales or *Craigslist* ads. Furnishings were all in good shape and although slight used, I reasoned that after even one short tenant they would be used. I shopped for quality and low-care items.

Even though the construction workers were only the summer months, in the winter I found another set of tenants. One such couple that rented for three winters were new to the state and were newly retired, they were enjoying camping and outdoor activities in the summers but moved into town and taught school in the winters. It was a great routine! Another couple worked fairs and camped during the summer months but were readily appreciative to move back into the same apartment.

Look for needs to fill and your units will be more prosperous.

Another demographic I marketed to were new-construction homebuyers. Generally new homebuilders must sell their home before they can close on the newly built home, and they are always in a time crunch and on a budget! Commonly last-minute expenses eat up the budgeted rental funds. People want to rent in between the moveout and move in, and fully furnished apartments fit their bill very well. But be warned, closing dates are estimated and can be extended, or are frequently shortened. It's all up in the air. Nevertheless, I learned to charge a deposit and a month's nonrefundable rent before I would accept their application, and they understood they were on the line for the first month's rent unless they could give one month's notice.

Too many times, I would get a call from an excited homebuyer, frequently in the early construction stages. They would call early and reserve an apartment. Their old home would be under contract and things would progress according to schedule. Once the home sells, the seller usually has a month to move, and the new home could be two to three months out. Dutifully, I would make the reservation and tell them to keep in touch. And they would! The excited happy calls came weekly—always good news: Now their new home was ahead of schedule, and they would only need one and a half months, then only one months and the final call: They would be closing within a week and since it was so short, their friends said they could sleep on their sofa! Although I wanted to cheer for them, I was the loser here! I learned to explain that they would only need to commit to one month, then with a minimum of a month's notice, they could end the tenancy, and receive their rent and their deposit, otherwise their prepaid month was not refundable! I found that worked very well.

Whether you choose to stay mainstream with your rentals of choose a niche, whatever route you choose to fill, versatility, or adaptability is the name of the game here. Try new things and work with the market. I really appreciated the versatility of the short-term renters once I made to switch, and furnishing the apartments was a creative outlet. I found in that particular economy there was a niche for it, and it made more money. People were willing to pay more for *not* having to commit to twelve months, although they may end up staying that long. People also paid more for furnishings—and moving was so much less of a hassle. People waiting on new construction would sign up with a deposit applied even two months early. People flying in to work a summer job would apply and pay a deposit beforehand also. It actually turned out to be pretty stable. My main concern was that I would have empty months, and if I did, I found it was welcomed as a great time to refurbish.

A young family with small children, may choose to owner occupy and open a daycare. This would definitely attract families with children needing daycare. This one really wasn't my cup of tea, but with the right location and conditions, I could see it working. With young families, you want the washer and dryer, playrooms, and fenced yards away from traffic.

WHO PAYS UTILITIES?

•	RENT	$ 1000	•	RENT	$ 850
•	UTILITIES	($300)	•	UTILITIES	$ 00
•	NET RENT	$ 750	•	NET RENT	$ 850

1031 Exchange

The Internal Revenue Code Section 1031 enables you to defer capital gains tax and depreciation recapture by reinvesting the proceeds from the sale of your investment property into a replacement property of *like-kind*, thus preserving the wealth in your estate. Your 1031 exchange deferrals can be continued through as many exchanges as you wish. If you sell the property without reinvesting in a new property, there will be capital gains and depreciation recapture tax liability.

A tax-deferred 1031 exchange can be a strong wealth-building tool. However, I highly recommend you consult a professional tax advisor to ensure that you meet every requirement of Internal Revenue Code Section 1031. Failure to comply with requirements can result in immediate tax liabilities and penalties. There is no room to mess around. You must strictly follow the strict timeline and procedural requirements for 1031 exchanges. Your title company or realtor can refer you to a professional exchange company.

On a 30-year mortgage, most of your mortgage payment after 15 years goes directly to your principal. You've seen the graph. If 91% of your first payment goes to interest, then 91% of your last payment goes to principal. The 15-year mark is where this is most apparent. After this more and more of your payment goes directly to principal. This is where the wealth you have built shows up. If you keep your property, it may be best to borrow or take out a second mortgage usually referred to as a *Home Equity Line of Credit* (HELOC) for any needed funds rather than sell or refinance and start the amortization over, since your equity is now more than half. Over the year this gradually increases, but while your payments were split between the principal, interest, insurance and taxes, your investment supported all that and you as it continued to grow. Not only do you have the value of the principal payments that over the years hammered down the mortgage debt, but if you have kept up the maintenance and taken good care of your property, it has appreciated. That's the thing about real estate, economies come and go but overall real estate always appreciates. People need housing.

After 20 years of owning and managing rental properties, which I thoroughly appreciated, I was ready to move on with my plan. Over the years, I'd had a few sleepless nights, and at times it felt like a wild ride downhill, over glare ice on a sled with metal runners. It's called *lickity-split* for a reason! I know what that feels like because as a child I tried it. Perhaps it left me a little bit head shy! Even so I was ready to move on. I sold my properties, quit my job and through a 1031 Exchange I was able to purchase my dream without tax penalties! I located a small resort in the small town where I was born, close to the highway and overlooking the bay. This will involve a few years to reach my potential, but I love it, and have to admit all my multifamily experience has helped considerably. Isn't this what it's all about? The life you build is what you end up with. It's a process. Jobs come and go but your life is always here. At the risk of sounding needlessly prophetic: This is your life—and this is one way to make the most of it.

IT'S A PROCESS!

Evelyn Harden

HelpSellHomes@mtaonline.net

Share experiences and advice

Everyone has something to learn & Everyone has something to share

The "school of hard knocks" can be avoided or enjoyed.

www.ingramcontent.com/pod-product-compliance
Lightning Source LLC
LaVergne TN
LVHW051128210926
848482LV00001B/21